The Modern Invention of Information

The

Modern
Invention
of
Information

Discourse, History, and Power

Ronald E. Day

Southern Illinois University Press
Carbondale and Edwardsville

Library of Congress Cataloging-in-Publication Data
Day, Ronald E., 1959–
The modern invention of information : discourse, history, and power / Ronald E. Day.
    p. cm.
Includes bibliographical references and index.
    1. Information society—History. 2. Information theory—History. 3. Information
theory in literature. 4. Information science—Philosophy—History. I. Title.

HM851 .D38 2001
306.4'2'09—dc21
                                            00-047033

ISBN 0-8093-2390-7 (alk. paper)

The paper used in this publication meets the minimum requirements of American National Standard for Information Sciences—Permanence of Paper for Printed Library Materials, ANSI Z39.48-1992. ♾

To Michael K. Buckland
In Admiration and Friendship

▪ Contents

▪ Acknowledgments

This book came out of a series of investigations into the history and social production of information and the information age, utilizing the resources of critical theory and centering on the role of professional, authoritative, and utopian rhetorics in this production. The people acknowledged below supported this project at different stages and share with me the belief that the history of information in modernity needs recovery and that the current social parameters for discussing information and knowledge need to be enlarged and to be more critical.

Barrett Watten, poet and theorist, helped inform some of the vocabulary and concepts in this book during the years I worked in the field of poetics. Robert Cooper of Keele University in England made it possible for me to explore the work of Pierre Lévy through an invitation to the Centre for Social Theory and Technology at Keele University during 1997. Yves Le Coadic of the Institut National des Techniques de la Documentation in Paris gave me an opportunity to coalesce thoughts on Suzanne Briet through an invited lecture with Michael Buckland at the INTD in December 1998. I have been fortunate to have Laurent Martinet of Paris as my co-translator of Suzanne Briet's *Qu'est-ce que la documentation?,* and some of the translated quotes from Briet's work in my book are from that co-translation. And last, Michael Buckland of the School of Information Management and Systems, University of California at Berkeley, to whom this book is dedicated, met with me for tea and discussion almost weekly from 1994 to 1999, providing source material and intellectual tools that are used throughout this work. I should add, as others would attest, that Michael's life has been not only that of an exemplary scholar, teacher, and administrator but also that of an extraordinarily generous and compassionate person.

I thank Mary Gray, currently in communications at the University of California at San Diego, Nina Wakeford in sociology at Surrey University (U.K.), and Steve Brown in psychology at the University of Lough-borough (U.K.) for their support of my work in the past and for valuable conversations that contributed to this book. I also thank several friends at, or formerly at, the University of Oklahoma, whose assistance and companionship were valuable to me during my stay in Norman during 1999–2000: Claire McInerney (Rutgers), who was a great support and whose comments on parts of this manuscript are very much appreciated; Francesca Novello for her patient work to improve my Italian; and Timothy S. Murphy, through whom my vocabulary and intellect were challenged and grew and who also was kind enough to comment on parts of this manuscript.

Though it came late in the composition of this text, I also acknowledge Jay Semel, director of the Obermann Center for Advanced Studies at the University of Iowa, and Lauren Rabinovitz and my other colleagues at the Digital Cultures seminar during June 2000 for their support and the discussion of the materials contained within this book.

I thank the readers of this manuscript during its review for their helpful comments; Karl Kageff, my editor at Southern Illinois University Press, for his work and support; Julie Bush for a superb job of copyediting; and Hermina Anghelescu (Wayne State) for supervising the indexing.

Finally, my thanks go to Mia and Pico, who were patiently next to me as I wrote through the night.

The Modern Invention of Information

1 ▪ Introduction: Remembering "Information"

> It is important for the materialist historian, in the most
> rigorous way possible, to differentiate the construction of a
> historical state of affairs from what one customarily calls its
> "reconstruction." The "reconstruction" in empathy is one-
> dimensional. "Construction" presupposes "destruction."
> —Walter Benjamin, *The Arcades Project*

I f we look in the *Oxford English Dictionary* under the term "information,"
we will be struck by the impression that its use as a substantive, as a syn-
onym for fact or for knowledge, is relatively new. Until very recently,
"information" had the sense of imparting knowledge (in the sense of
telling someone something) or of giving sensory knowledge (in the way
that our senses inform us of some event). For us late moderns, however,
information has now become a thing, and not only but also an eco-
nomically valuable thing. Why is this so, how did it come to happen, and
what are its consequences, particularly now, in the so-called information
age? How did we arrive at this reified and commodified notion of knowledge or of becoming informed? And what have we forgotten in this historical process?

This book is about vocabulary and its role in constructing and producing history. In particular, this book is concerned with the social production and history of the term "information": how the term and its connotations became an important social and epistemic value for Western society
of the twentieth century and how that evaluation came (and comes) to
construct a historical future that we all must live with into the twenty-first
century. This book, however, is also about those critical elements of historical agency that attempted to speak about information and communication technologies in some other manner than a determined future. This
book not only tells of three information ages but also attempts to recover

different, riskier historical engagements with information culture and ideology such as occurred in Europe in the late 1930s.

In this book, I examine texts of three information ages: European documentation before and soon after World War II, United States information theory and cybernetics soon after World War II, and the "virtual" age that is proclaimed today. I attempt to show how professional and authoritative texts about the social importance of information tried to use language (particularly through books) to construct a social, utopian value for information and helped to raise information and its connotations of factuality and quantitative measure to a privileged, even totalitarian, form of knowledge and discourse. I also attempt to show how a popular "scientific" or authoritative meaning of information has been constructed by rhetorical devices and how the notion of an "information age" has been, since the beginning of the twentieth century, a futurological trope used for professional self-advancement.

In trying to restore a context of literary, social, and historical production to "information," we are forced to account for the social, professional, and textual means through which information is produced, presented, and deployed as a historical form. In this book, I have chosen to focus largely on the textual means of information's historical development, because, in my view, textual accounts are sometimes best able to account for the movement of concepts *across* institutionally defined social networks. Through a historically conscious rhetorical analysis, I believe that one can account for the powerful ability of vocabulary to construct cultural and social histories. That we can point to three information ages that utilize similar diction and tropes to proclaim the "newness" of their ages suggests that the historical and social cycles of remembering and forgetting, which mark each of these ages, involve rhetorical devices that leverage language and history toward creating the present and the future. If, as I believe, *the history of information is a privileged site for understanding the intersection of language and political economy in modernity,* then an analysis of the history of information first of all involves the untangling of the language of information and its ideological supports and interests.

No historical account of information in the twentieth century can turn away from the problem of how a rhetoric, an aesthetic, and, consequently, an ideology of information has come to shape late modern history and historiography. As a high school librarian at the historical moment when online access became widely available, I witnessed a revolution in how students understood the meaning of "history" based on the rhetoric and aesthetics of on-line digital texts. "Doing" historical study for these students became a matter of cutting and pasting informational texts, a process many times faster than any sense of *reading* itself. It may be objected, of course, that these students were not really "doing" historical research, because they were not working with difficult primary documents in relatively unknown historical contexts. This is true, but in terms of creating an *informational sense of history*—what might be thought of in one sense as a *popular* history—informational bits of history were exactly what was needed to create the narrative, causal illusion of a true "history." In a very real social and political sense, these students were creating and recreating an informational history from informational documents of history. This sense of filling in a narrative of history with informational facts or "sound bytes" is not so different from what information utopians have done within the narrative forms of technical determinism or capitalist global destiny. In both Heidegger's sense of metaphysics and Benjamin's sense of commodity or of nationalist aura, the popular sense of information in twentieth-century modernity has often acted as a trope for the dominant ideological narrative within which culture, society, and knowledge are represented and projected.

My argument is not only that the history of information has been forgotten but also that it *must be forgotten* within any "metaphysics" or ideology of information, because information in modernity connotes a factuality and pragmatic presence (what Heidegger in *Being and Time* termed a "present-at-hand" *[vorhanden]* quality) that erases or radically reduces ambiguity and the problems of reading, interpreting, and constructing history—problems that are intrinsic not only to historiographic construction but also to historical agency.

The main argument of my book is divided into four chapters. The second, third, and fourth chapters examine texts that use rhetorical devices to produce reified and commodified notions of information. The fifth chapter examines attempts at intervening in this process of social and historical abstraction and production in 1930s Europe and later. The last chapter concludes with some thoughts on the relation of a critical theory to the rhetoric and concept of information in late modernity.

In chapter 2, I attempt to sketch some of the rhetorical strategies that early European documentalists used for expanding the social meaning of the technical treatment of documents into the world on a global scale. The second chapter also examines the rhetoric of "science" in European documentation and how that rhetoric worked in the social expansion of a professional understanding of technique.

The third chapter examines attempts at the expansion of "information theory" into social space after World War II, particularly in the writings of Warren Weaver and Norbert Wiener. In this chapter, I suggest that this expansion was driven by Cold War political motivations and by a reactionary humanism. Toward the end of that chapter, I propose a sense of community different from that which Weaver's and Wiener's understanding of information leads to, one based on an older concept of information as affect rather than as reified "fact."

Chapter 4 examines the work of the contemporary French theorist Pierre Lévy on virtual identity and community. Lévy's work reflects earlier expansions of technical norms and vocabulary into social space but now within a rhetoric of "cyberspace" and the "virtual." As I will show, Lévy's use of the term "virtual" demonstrates how popular tropes for information form what we might call ideological "strong attractors" for redefining earlier historical works, events, and vocabulary. Lévy appropriates the term "virtual" and other related concepts from earlier works by, particularly, Gilles Deleuze and Félix Guattari, and he makes this vocabulary perform ideological and historiographical tasks that are, at times, quite opposite those intended by the original authors. Lévy's work performs a similar but more pronounced appropriation of language, history, and culture for the purposes of professional and political capitalization and control than that performed by the European documentalists and by Weaver's and Wiener's popular writings. His work casts an interesting light on the information age's ability to bend history and social space through the prisms of ideology.

The fifth chapter introduces modernist attempts at critical intervention into the construction of an information culture. In this chapter, I examine theories of the production of information and information culture from the aspect of a critique of metaphysics (Martin Heidegger) and from the aspect of a formalist Marxist critique (Walter Benjamin). The purpose of this chapter is to recover historically forgotten critical interventions of "information" that attempted to examine and exploit those processes of reproduction through which information is reified and commodified, both as a concept and as actual values, and through which it becomes a historical force.

Throughout this work, it is my desire to expose the process by which language passes through the machinery of authoritative rhetorical devices and institutions for the purposes of ideological control. Professional discourses, particularly in management, organizational theory, and information science, sometimes contain rhetorical edifices built upon tropes such as "Information Management," "Knowledge Management," and "Information Architecture." The attempt in this book is to put critical pressure on professionally and politically based reifications and commodifications of language and to demonstrate some of the plays of power and ideology that are involved in the rhetorical and aesthetic capitalization and exploitation of human relations and affects in the names of "information" and "communication."

It is my hope that this book constitutes one text in an increasing series of critical interventions into the "information society." Particularly in the United States—partly due to the vast concentration of wealth in military and corporate research and partly due to the subsequent willful ignorance of Marxist, nonquantitative, non-"practical," and, largely, non-American analyses of information—analyses of information and society and culture have almost totally been given over to so-called information specialists and public policy planners, mainly from computer science, business and business schools, the government, and the quantitative social sciences. This concentration has led to a focus on quantitative methods of analysis, a neglect of critical modes and vocabularies for analysis, a dependence on naive historiographical forms for analyzing the phenomenon of information, and a neglect of art and culture outside of conceptions of historical transmission (that is, "cultural heritage"). The overwhelming trend has been to place responsibility for the creation of an "information society" into ideologically conformist, "professional" hands, which inhibits truly critical analyses and discussions where the fundamental premises and political stakes of information and communication might be shown and put into question.

I would ask that these last remarks be understood not as mere complaints about the present but as concerns about how a future might be imagined and lived. For what this book traces is a tendency toward an increasingly uncritical and idealistic history and a speculative relation to historical and political agency. In many ways, the death of materialist analysis and of personal agency in the twentieth century follows the rise of the ideology of information. And with this death, the struggles, affects, and language of individual lives lose their power within the categories of acceptable meaning.

The original title for this book was *Where Do You Want to Go Tomorrow?*, which was a pun on Microsoft's late-1990s ad campaign, "Where Do You Want to Go Today?" Given that the latter phrase is owned as a Microsoft trademark, and given that Microsoft has, apparently, in the past threatened to sue others for the use of the *former* phrase as well as the latter, I decided not to use that title. This situation, I think, speaks loudly of the problems of ownership and control of language and history by dominant players in information and communication technologies. We need to take language and historical agency back and thus take back from the information and communication technology "prophets" and profits their determination of our todays and our tomorrows. I hope that this book will be one part of this critical *praxis* in its attempt to demystify the trope of information in modern culture.

2 ▪ European Documentation: Paul Otlet and Suzanne Briet

European Documentation

The active history of European documentation spans the years from the founding of the International Institute of Bibliography by Paul Otlet and Henri Lafontaine in 1895 in Brussels to its eclipse by information science after World War II. Though European documentation still exists in the form of such organizations as the Fédération Internationale de Documentation, the period just before and after World War II saw the publication of several defining texts by leading figures in documentation: the *Traité de documentation* (1934) and *Monde* (1935) by Paul Otlet and the small but important manifesto by Suzanne Briet, *Qu'est-ce que la documentation?* (1951). The distinguishing characteristic of documentation in Europe, in contrast to both librarianship in Europe and to what would subsequently become information science in the United States, was the manner in which documentation understood the relationship between information technology and social systems. For documentation, the technical retrieval of materials was deeply tied to the social and institutional use and goals for documentary materials. In contrast to the functions of libraries and librarians, which defined themselves in terms of the historical collection and preservation of books, documentalists emphasized the utilitarian integration of technology and technique toward specific social goals.

The founders and leaders of European documentation were advocates of documentation as an upcoming profession, distinct from librarianship, based both within and serving the development of science in modernity. As an organized system of techniques and technologies, documentation was understood as a player in the historical development of global organization in modernity—indeed, a major player inasmuch as that organization was dependent on the organization and transmission of information. It was within the context of a "scientific" culture of modernity that documentation could be understood as not simply bibliographical technique but as a cultural technique.

Insofar as the foundational texts of documentation proclaim that documentation is both a symptom and a producer of modernist culture, it is important to examine these texts not only for their historical influence on later developments in information technology and information science but also as symptoms of the birth of a culture of information. From these texts, we can identify not only the early forms of later technological inventions but also tropes and rhetorical strategies that have been used up to the present time in the advocacy and prediction of an "information age." Though the foundational texts of documentation have a historical specificity, they also share with our own time modernist characterizations about information and its relation to culture. This repetition in the twentieth century of rhetorical tropes about the information age is important, for in each case we witness not only a group of authors' intentions to advance an information profession or technology's social stature and goals but also the production and use of cultural rhetorics and institutions that aid the achievement of such intentions. The continuity or tradition of such use and production constitutes the historical culture of information in modernity.

The dialectic between professional discourses and cultural discourses helps determine the meaning and the historical development of genera of technologies that are named by the terms "information technologies" and "communication technologies," or, more recently, "information and communication technologies" (ICTs). This dialectic also works toward developing related professions through the development of culture at large. The study of such "professional" texts thus reveals more than a concern with a narrow professionalism. There is also a global cultural vision that, in the case of European documentation, joined and was shared by the visions of such global organizations as the League of Nations and the United Nations Educational, Scientific, and Cultural Organization (UNESCO). If it were the case that professional texts were not both constituting and constituted by cultural histories, then their self-narratives and their historical prophecies for society as a whole would be of little significance. But inasmuch as professional texts do utilize dominant cultural tropes and desires for their professional interest, they synthesize those tropes and desires that project the most positive light on their profession, giving to themselves positive historical value.

In what follows in this chapter, I discuss the dialectic between the professional discourse of European documentation and pre- and postwar modernist culture. I concentrate on texts written by the founder of European documentation, Paul Otlet, and some postwar texts of "Madame Documentation," Suzanne Briet. With Otlet's work, attention is focused on certain representative sections of his magnum opus, *Traité de documentation: le livre sur le livre: théorie et pratique* (1934).

Paul Otlet and the Machinations of World Peace

As Serge Cacaly writes in *Dictionnaire encyclopédique de l'information et de la documentation,* Paul Otlet (1868–1944) may be considered the founder of information science and of European documentation.[1] Such a claim is justified because Otlet's writings and professional work not only envisioned later technical innovations but also—and more important— projected a global vision for information and information technologies that speaks directly to postwar visions of a global "information society." Alone and together with Henri Lafontaine (who won the Nobel Peace Prize in 1913), Otlet was instrumental in setting up numerous professional organizations dedicated to standardization, bibliography, international associations, and consequently, international cooperation. These organizations were foundational for assuring international production and commerce, information, communication, and modern economic development, and they eventually found their global form in such institutions as the League of Nations and, later, the United Nations.

Otlet's vision was exemplary in that it spanned the breadth and paradoxes of modernist notions of information across the nineteenth and twentieth centuries. Otlet was the designer of a comprehensive classification scheme for international use based on Melvil Dewey's decimal classification system (the Universal Decimal Classification) but was also an advocate of more flexible, systems-based standards for information retrieval. He was a proponent of the central cultural importance of the book but also a proponent of radio and cinema in their displacement of the book. He was a theologian of a unified, positive science but also a practitioner of a documentary technique based on small "atomic" chunks of text and the networking of those chunks into paper-based, proto-hypertext documents. Most of all, Otlet was an enthusiastic advocate for a type of world peace founded on nineteenth-century notions of "scientific" progress and European-dominated global unity, and yet he was also a disappointed optimist as World War II approached, with a bitter understanding of the limitations of knowledge. Otlet's foundational role in establishing European documentation is undeniable, as is the importance of documentation and its allied associations in shaping information policies and culture between the two world wars in Europe.

Otlet's understanding of documentation was expressed through his trope of "the book," which Otlet variously referred to as the book *(le livre)*, the book-document *(le livre-document)*, the document, and generically as *"le Biblion."* Otlet's trope of the book referred to both the physical object of the book and, even more importantly, to a cultural concept of the book as a unifying form for positive knowledge. Inasmuch as this concept not only embodies the physical object of the book but also is reflective of social and natural "facts," it represented for Otlet a concrete embodiment of the history of true knowledge and is thus a vehicle to global understanding.

Otlet's interreading of the textual and the social was possible, and indeed necessary, on the basis of the privilege that Otlet gives to the destiny and the problem of "man" in his writings on the technique and social necessity of documentation.[2] The philosophical problem of the "question of man" arose in relation to the problem of the certainty of nonscriptural knowledge in the eighteenth century and forms the backdrop for Otlet's documentary quest. Bibliographical "laws" and physical laws, for example, come together in Otlet's work around the central problem of man's historical development through informational knowledge. In Otlet's professional works, particularly in his *Traité de documentation,* metaphor and hyperbole abound, giving to his professional texts a highly determinate social element that attempts to reach beyond the present toward shaping the future. By means of literary devices, Otlet's text goes beyond its own time, projecting humanity into a future that Otlet desired to create, both through information technologies and techniques and through the very rhetorical force of his texts.

The tropic quality of what we might call "informational objects," such as the book, is noteworthy in Otlet's work, because it is a quality that runs throughout "visionary" texts about information, whether that privileged device be the book or, as Paul N. Edwards has noted, "the computer." In Otlet's writings, "the book" stands for facts, documents, physical books, and knowledge as information or "science," and in turn, each of these signifiers refers back to the culture of the book. This trope, embodying Otlet's understanding of knowledge and history, found its architectural embodiment in Otlet's vision of a world city, the Cité Mondiale, which he attempted to establish, with Le Corbusier's architectural designs, in Geneva (Gresleri). For Otlet, both book and city were to be "a reproduction, an abridgement, a synthesis of all the best that Humanity can produce" (*Monde* 333). Far from being an antiquated vision, the metaphorical and metonymical power of the book in architecture's construction of social space continues to our own day, even with institutions whose claim is to have entered the "digital age." Nor is Otlet's notion of the book antiquated by today's hypertext: it was that of a whole with multiple, interconnected parts, a forerunner of hypertextual linking following what Otlet termed the "monographic principle" (that is, "atomic" chunks of text).[3] Rhetorically, as well as technologically, the book moves diachronically back and forth through twentieth-century culture, tracing and retracing a culture of knowledge and social control marked by a dialectic between global unification and local networks. This cultural trope of the book thus not only reflected but also shaped the meaning and development of information and communication technologies in the twentieth century as well as the meaning of those technologies in social space and as a symbol for social space.

Otlet's work was "visionary" because he situated his writings within the dominant terms of a dialectic between technical and professional culture and the larger culture of modernity. Otlet was part of a large historical and ideological current even as his own idiosyncrasies and insistence on particular technologies and goals for documentation were sometimes viewed as strange by librarians as well as by supporting government institutions of the time. As a trope for architectural, social, and natural orders, the book constitutes, at least since the sixteenth century, an exemplary instance of the ability of one technology, raised by institutions and rhetoric to a cultural level, to historically and socially organize other series of bodies, technologies, and actions. In this, the book foreshadowed the cultural rhetoric of the digital computer in post–World War II industrial societies. In Otlet's writings, the book emerges in all its rhetorical splendor, highlighting the metaphysical, historical, and rhetorical genealogies that would infuse the social meaning of later technologies, such as radio, film, television, and, in our own day, the internet.

Not only through a technological regime but also through the circulation of rhetorical tropes between wider cultural domains, technologies emerge in both design and social meaning. Cultural metaphors act as influences on technological designs (for example, computers should act like the mind) that then, in turn, influence larger cultural realms (for example, the mind should act with the instrumentality of a computer). Rhetorical diffusion leads to technological design, development, and acceptance as well as to the shaping of culture according to technological models. Tropes of technology, and especially of information, not only metaphorically repeat themselves through different domains of culture but also metonymically leverage history, forcing societies to develop according to "inevitable" technological models.

The literary nature of Otlet's professional writings is a quality shared by many other visionary texts about the operation, role, and meaning of information and communication technologies. Rather than this quality being seen as a violation of "science," however, it is precisely what allows Otlet's texts to reach beyond a narrow professional realm and into the future. In addition, as I suggest throughout this book, this type of literary quality is what makes information what it is within twentieth- and early-twenty-first-century modernist culture.

Hyperbole in a text can be subtle or loud; in Otlet's text it is deafening. In contrast to more subtle uses of literary devices, Otlet's enthusiasm and his tendency toward overstatement and vast generalization give to his texts a level of honesty and, yet, critical vulnerability. Unlike some other works I examine in this book, Otlet's work is filled with historical risks. His desire for world peace was such that he did not mince words. Despite whatever analytical flaws are evident in Otlet's writings, they display an integrity that is as admirable as it is tragic in its clear failures. These qualities give his writings a rhetorical boldness that is worth examining not only for biographical reasons but, more important, to analyze the social and cultural values that informed prewar documentation, information, and information and communication technologies.

Given the importance that the political future had for Otlet's understanding of the book and bibliography, and given that the book plays an important figurative role in the founding and renewal of concepts of culture in modernity, it is instructive to look in more detail at exactly what constitutes Otlet's concept of the book. For just as the book constitutes Otlet's hope for a universal or global future, so this figure is also composed of tropes from Otlet's present, foremost from Otlet's appropriation of a rhetoric of science in his day.

How far the book (and its successors) constitutes a trope upon which the future can be determined is perhaps not a task for the historian alone but for the cultural critic as well, since the trope of the book occupies a series of rhetorical substitutions not only in historiography but in culture at large, which claims "the future" for itself. What is at stake in reexamining the texts of information proponents, such as Otlet, is the right of a certain produced sense of information to claim our future.

Though it is often claimed that the tropes of the book and of information constitute two sides of a historical caesura marked by the advent of digital processors, Otlet's work is a nice example of the unhistorical nature of such a claim. The histories of the book and that of information are neither continuous nor discontinuous with one another, but rather they form a line of historical meaning that shapes a tradition of information culture. In the following analyses, we will see how Otlet reads the rather traditional concept of the book in terms of a dynamic systems approach according to the "laws" of positive science. Later, we will see how Otlet's implicit understanding of the role that such bibliographical (or as he sometimes puts it, "bibliological") laws have in service to society is made explicit in Suzanne Briet's proclamation that documentation is a "cultural technique." What each of these authors sought to do was to expand the social meaning and importance of documentation and information, and they did this through the use of literary devices in professional and semi-professional authoritative texts on documentation and information.

Energy, Transformation, and Renewal

In the section of the *Traité* entitled "Bibliographical Laws" (section 51), Otlet explains bibliographical law in terms of the laws of other sciences as applied to the particular form and agency of the physical book. This section in the *Traité* is an important one, as it presents a basic ontology of the book and its relation to those scientific "facts" that are articulated within its covers. Consequently, Otlet defines information and documentation through their mimetic and metonymical relationship to science, a model that runs through documentation and information theory, whether science denotes knowledge as facts, as systems, or as transmission.

In this chapter of the *Traité,* Otlet conceptualizes the book as a container of knowledge. Knowledge for Otlet is a substance in the form of facts, and facts flow between the world, books, and thinkers in a circulating manner. Consequently, Otlet's understanding of the book simultaneously encompasses three models: an organism, a dynamic embodiment of energy (which Otlet often refers to as *l'esprit* [mind or spirit]), and a machine of production.

Otlet's organic conception of the book draws on a classical tradition that goes back to Aristotle and is found in neoclassical and romantic rules for the formal unity of creative works in the late eighteenth and early nineteenth centuries. What is interesting in Otlet's thought, however, is how this classical organicism then incorporates systems theory through appeals to mechanical functions, ecological energy flows, and physical laws. Otlet's work, thus, brings early bibliographical organicism into the twentieth century by incorporating within the trope of the book generalizations of scientific laws and facts.

For Otlet, the part-whole organic form of the book functions like a machine. This requires, of course, that there be a consideration of processes of production, inputs, and outputs. Despite having a formal structure that is unitary and singular, Otlet's book-organism is not closed and self-contained in its origins and future. Instead, the bibliographical "law of organization" suggests that books contain and constitute networks or webs *("réseau"),* both internally and externally in their relations with one another and to the world at large (*Traité* 423). The concept of *réseau* is very important for Otlet because it designates not only the internal structure of the book itself but also the relation of books to one another, to facts, and to thought. At its inner parameter, along with the model of the machine, it signifies the functional and generative interaction of words, phrases, sentences, and other grammatical elements within the book. At its outer parameter, it is a term that signifies universal or global collections, whether in the form of paper codices, bibliographies, museum collections, electronic networks, or, at the most extreme, the *"biblion"* of all these mediums in relation to one another.

Otlet conceives of the expansion of the book's intellectual totality in terms of historically determined social systems of input, production, and output. For Otlet, books are part of an evolutionary process of thought, and as such, books contain what came before them in other books. The manner of this evolution from one book to another is very specific: it occurs in terms of *"répétition"* (423). Repetition, for Otlet, is a universal law of not simply repeating the same with the same result, but it is a peculiar type of repeating that is characterized as an amplification (*"La loi de répétition amplifiante"* [422]). Repetition, as an amplification, leads to the universal and "geometric" expansion of knowledge (422). Such an expansion suggests that there is a change of scale for the nature and value of knowledge. For Otlet, texts are both vehicles and embodiments of dynamic repetition, leading to an expansion of knowledge and to a change in the form of knowledge.

Otlet's conception of the social and historical attributes of texts thus demands that texts be understood in terms of their networked and evolutionary relations to one another and, subsequently, that knowledge be understood in terms of these relations. For Otlet, texts are networked to one another in terms of historical influence and interpretation, and external organizational devices, such as the Universal Decimal Classification system, are explicit acknowledgments of shared genealogies and historical alliances.

For Otlet, the evolutionary development of the world through knowledge is related to the expansion of knowledge through books and other documentary forms. Evolution is both progressive and paradigmatic. Any particular book, for Otlet, is an example of a specific historical object whose unique meaning is contingent on the historical past and the evolving future. Otlet's containment of bibliographical historicity within the notion of scientific laws, however, means that Otlet's vision of the book and of the world is highly deterministic. The evolution of knowledge follows the laws of progress even as the effect of books on one another may be revolutionary. Moments of ideational completion lead only to higher degrees of expansion and then completeness based on the accumulation of scientific facts and their linkage through universal bibliography (430).

For Otlet, bibliography's law of repetition follows the physical-chemical laws of the transformation of energy. Books conserve or embody "thought-energy." Bibliographical energy, for Otlet, is the mental energy of thought that is the content of books. Energy in books is stored, transformed, and produced through the historically specific form of each book as it functions as a "book-machine" in social and bibliographical networks. For Otlet, the book has both repository and generative functions. The mental energy of thought is contained, produced, and liberated by means of the book.

Even as books are productive and transformative, for Otlet they are also points of equilibrium in the circulation of energy, which is historically conservative in its tendency to transform rather than lose knowledge. The conservative nature of Otlet's "bibliographical law" points to the presence of an original repository of knowledge in nature that lies behind the repository of individual books and awaits discovery. As mental representations of fact, thought is neither created nor destroyed but instead evolves to make facts more clear and true. Books, as containers of knowledge, follow positive science in their task of revealing the facts of the universe:

> The law of the conservation of energy: never lost, never created, all is transformation. In the book also: books conserve mental energy, what is contained in books passes to other books when they themselves have been destroyed; and all bibliological[4] creation, no matter how original and how powerful, implies redistribution, combination and new amalgamations from what is previously given. (422–23)

When Otlet attempts to illustrate the flow of mental energy in bibliographical systems, he often uses examples from natural ecology such as the circulation of water through rivers, seas, and clouds in the process of rain evaporation and condensation. Analogous with natural ecological systems, the book is part of "the chain of operations of production, distribution, conservation, utilization, and destruction" (423). In making such analogies, Otlet points both toward future systems theory and back toward natural classification systems of the eighteenth century that, in attempting to encompass all of fauna and flora in the book of God's creation, brought the natural world into hierarchical and comparative orders of classification. Otlet's bibliographical analogies with natural systems are, thus, modern extensions of a tradition of analogical and representational comparisons between objects of nature and objects of knowledge that run throughout positive science, and his understanding of intertwining systems of knowledge and fact in thought is an attempt to bridge the hermeneutic difficulties of positive science.

The circulation of information flows between conjoining but different types of information systems is a common conception in postwar systems analysis and cybernetics. But Otlet's earlier application of systems theory to the cultural trope of the book is not so obvious, because at a physical level, paper material, especially in bound form, has a substantial resistance to practices of heterogeneous linkage. In order to understand how Otlet came to incorporate systems and network theory into the historical trope of the book, one must consider Otlet's own documentary work on books and other documents.

As W. Boyd Rayward has suggested, the practical origins for Otlet's theoretical concept of the "monographic principle" was Otlet's practice of breaking complex textual elements into simpler, molecular forms, which were then linked together as a data base by means of the Universal Decimal Classification system. Rayward writes, "The idea was to 'detach' what the book amalgamates, to reduce all that is complex to its elements and to devote a page [that is, card] to each" ("Origins" 295) and then link the cards into a larger structure. Otlet's practice of breaking down the material book into atomic units through the use of note cards and then rebuilding it through a classificatory metalanguage literally opened the traditional closure of the book and reassembled it within expanding universes of knowledge. Otlet's subsequent theoretical conception of the book as a machine in historical and social economies of knowledge thus owes at least part of its origin to this practice, which in its formal design and its level of "chunking" text bears some resemblance to digital hypertext systems. For Otlet, the monograph was, thus, a node within a system of linkages, which together formed the larger idea of the monograph or "book" of all universal knowledge. The "monographic principle" was both a curious extension of cultural assumptions about the book and a literal destruction of the book in its traditional physical form.

It is important to note here the manner through which cultural rhetorics mediated a relationship between theory and practice so that the documentary profession could appear as both a science and a practice and thus fulfill the social expectations for a mature profession in modernity. Popular positivist assumptions and vocabulary about science provided Otlet with the tropes of facts, atomic elements, laws, and energy circulation that are the theoretical vocabulary through which Otlet explained and socially validated his bibliographical practice. This borrowing of tropes from popular understandings of science lent to Otlet's theoretical writings an air of being "scientific," making, at least rhetorically, European documentation an early "information science." In turn, the value of "science" within modern culture gave documentation a basis for claiming an avant-garde position in society, a position that Otlet hoped would lead to social progress and world peace. The point is that the circulation of tropes from popular conceptions of science to nascent information science had not only technological implications in justifying and extending Otlet's practical application of the "monographic principle" but political and social ones as well.

Since the agency of the book is so important in Otlet for developing the "scientific" laws of thought, let us look a little closer at Otlet's conception of the "book-machine." For however bizarre Otlet's book-machine may appear, it envisions systems theories for information and present-day understandings of the virtual community.

The Book-Machine

Otlet's understanding of the book as a transformative agency for mental energy is embodied in his metaphor of the book as a machine. As with his term "the book," the term "book-machine" refers to paper documents as well as other types of objects that may be understood as containing or transmitting thought. Otlet's citation of Archimedes' famous statement points to a functional characterization of documents as well as to Otlet's belief that documents can "geometrically" change the relation of a given body of knowledge to the world:

> The mechanism which studies or which produces the
> application of the mechanical is a combination of organs
> or parts disposed for the production of a functional as-

semblage. The Book is a mechanism, a dynamism, and to it one is also given to apply the words of Archimedes:
"Da mihi ubi consistarrs et terram loco dimouebo" [*sic*].
"Give me a fulcrum and I will move the earth." (422)

Analogous to an organism being analyzed in terms of its agency within an ecological system, the book-machine is connected to other books and other organic "machines," forming systemic assemblages in the conservation and transformation of mental energy throughout history. Otlet explains in the *Traité* that machines are extensions *("prolongement")* of the human body. As transformational organisms, machines not only aid the human body but also replace and intensify it (*"Le but de la machine est d'aider, remplacer ou intensifier la puissance de l'homme"* [387]). It is because the book-machine transforms the human body by being a supplement to it that Otlet asks, for example, what detrimental effects books may have upon the brain over time, even though Otlet claims that books save the brain from a form of mental "explosion" in the brain's attempt to comprehend the explosion of information in the modern world. The book is both the mechanism of producing this explosion and the means for controlling it, thus giving to modern man a tool that is related to the human organism yet stands beyond it in a bibliographical totality as a sort of "world mind":

> *The Book as an Instrument of Abstraction*—As this type of mechanism, the book is a condensed intellectual force that, in the manner of steam, electricity, and gunpowder, which, with a small material volume, after ignition and release, produces a considerable expansive force in the brain. The mechanism of the book realizes the means for creating the reserves of intellectual forces: it is an accumulator [*accumulateur:* literally, a battery]. Exteriorization of the brain itself, the book develops to the detriment of the brain as tools develop to the detriment of the body. In his development, man, in place of acquiring new senses, new organs (for example, three eyes, six ears, four noses), has developed his brain by abstraction, the latter by the sign, and the sign by the book. (426)

Books are, thus, supplementary tools to the body. They serve not only to store but to transform and output thought through mechanical "transcription." Otlet's language shows an obvious fascination with the ability of the book to be a hybrid, cyborg object. It is both a part of the human organism and also a sort of computational machine within its own order. As such, Otlet's conception of the book and universal bibliography fore-shadows mental metaphors for digital computers and computer networks as technological forms of a "world brain" (as Otlet, Wilhelm Ostwald, H. G. Wells, and others of the time put it).[5]

Beyond being a supplemental agency to the body, however, books for Otlet are transformative of individual sensory information. They stretch thought out beyond itself to a totality that is made possible by inscription: "And as an intellectual instrument, the book serves not only to state theories, but to construct them; not only to translate thought, but to form it. It sees opening before it all the destined brilliance of its mechanical transcription" (426).

For Otlet, the book-machine forms networked and hybrid relations with other organisms, transforming the energy of those organisms through its own historical specificity. The book-machine can do this, however, because it already has the ability to absorb mental energy from other organisms in its environment. As both accumulator and transformer, the book is neither a singular organism nor is it simply part of a whole. As an accumulator, the book-machine contains the multiplicity of the world before it. As a transformer, it is a productive agency within an ecology of affects. These two aspects simultaneously point the book toward an older cultural understanding of books (which saw books and libraries as repositories for knowledge) and toward a more modern model for information technology that sees documentary forms as productive agents in the networked creation of information products and flows.

Otlet's vision is Platonic, and even Hegelian, in that it proposes the unfolding of reason through history. The agencies for this unfolding, however, are not the great events in history (as in Hegel's systems of philosophy) but the representations and the productive transmission of all the facts of the world to, potentially, all the people of the world through information and communication technologies.

This is brought out in Otlet's book *Monde,* where "the ultimate problem of documentation" is envisioned: the creation of a technological device that would unify information but also transform it in such a way as to present it in the most "advantageous" manner to each viewer. The final goal of such a project would be the presentation of all the "facts" of existence to all the people—a sort of Hegelian vision of absolute being with information playing the role of Hegel's notion of truth. Epistemic "transformation," here, ends with a form of total representation. History, for

Otlet, was a progressive movement of ever-accumulating knowledge and clarity; what was lacking was a device for the storage, retrieval, and communication of this progressive store so as to bring the fruits of reason to all the citizens of the world. Otlet's multimedia device would present to each person, in the comfort of his or her own armchair, something like the omniscient vision of the world by God. At one stroke, this device would solve the problem of science (to rationally represent all things in the world), the problem of technique (to rationally organize all the knowledge of the world), and the problem of society (to make available to each person all the knowledge of the world) (390). For these lofty ends, Otlet envisioned a multimedia device that, "acting at a distance . . . would combine the radio, x-rays, cinema, and microscopic photography," projecting the information of the world onto an "individual screen." Such a device would provide each person with a true and complete picture of all knowledge in a manner that would be most true for each person, thus eliminating conflicts over differing interpretations and providing the grounds for "true" conversation. Such a device "would become the liberator of each person, its operation being controlled by each person himself, and the things [in their representations] being placed in a convenient order for each person['s] understanding" (390–91).

Otlet's vision thus culminates with a unification of informational multiplicity in an aesthetically representational form delivered through what we might today see as a "multimedia" computer. Otlet's envisioned technological device involves an aesthetic that claims to be able to bring the facts of the world to all people in the comfort of their own dwellings. The legacy of this vision remains for us today in the notion of a global community made present on a personal computer screen. Inasmuch as this global information is embodied not just in the contents of representation but also in common standards for technology and for aesthetic forms through which the real may be both recognized as such and customized for distributed presentation and understanding, we may come to see Otlet's vision of documentation as a vision for a society in which standardization—technological, aesthetic, and psychological—is the necessary condition for all true knowledge.

As we will now see, in Suzanne Briet's writings these tendencies are expressed within the trope of industrial "science." Briet believes that science must be spread throughout the "undeveloped" world through a union of technique and technology in documentation. Later, in chapter 3, we will see both Otlet's and Briet's visions of a totally communicative community repeated in Pierre Lévy's vision of what he claims is an inevitable world of the "virtual" that we are entering into today.

Briet's Antelope

Suzanne Briet (1894–1989), nicknamed "Madame Documentation," was one of the foremost leaders in early documentation just before and after World War II. Her publications ranged from the small but extremely important book *Qu'est-ce que la documentation?* to work on her relative, the nineteenth-century poet Arthur Rimbaud, to an autobiography that is formally composed, in an avant-garde manner, according to alphabetical entries. Professionally, she was one of the first women librarians at the Bibliothèque Nationale, and she created and was in charge of the Salle des Catalogues et des Bibliographies at that library from 1934 to 1954. She was active in international circles, acting as vice president of the International Federation for Documentation and president of the Union of European Women, holding assignments with UNESCO, and taking a Fulbright-supported tour of libraries in the United States toward the end of her career as a librarian. In 1937, Briet attended the World Congress on Universal Documentation in Paris, which was also attended by Paul Otlet, H. G. Wells, and other notables who were interested in world bibliography (Rayward, "International Exposition"). Briet was not only a central figure in European documentation; her publications show her to be critically aware of the problems of formal technique in writing (for example, her autobiography) as well as aware of contemporary developments in American cybernetics (which she praises in *Qu'est-ce que la documentation?*) (Buckland, "Centenary").

For Otlet, "the book" was a trope for scientific positivism and the term "science" itself was a trope for future social-political organization; in Briet's writings after World War II, culture as a whole is now scientific, in the form of industrial production, and documentation is both a reflection of science and a leader of science. Throughout Briet's professional writings, foremost in the third chapter of *Qu'est-ce que la documentation?*, documentation is referred to as "a technique for our time" or a "cultural technique for our time."

What, then, is this technique that is documentation, and how, as so often occurs with information techniques and technologies, does documentary technique not only belong to a scientific time but also then becomes characterized as a symbol of science? In what follows, I will examine the tropic displacements that occur between "science" and "documentation" in Briet's texts and will show how the technique of indexing becomes a central figure in Briet's texts for not only representing the nature and role of documentation within postwar science but also for explaining science itself in terms of networks of production. I will do this by examining two of Briet's most important works on documentation, her book *Qu'est-ce que la documentation?* and her article "Bibliothécaires et documentalistes," published in 1954 in *Revue de documentation.*

Science and the Problem of Evidence

Briet opens her manifesto on documentation, *Qu'est-ce que la documentation?,* in a somewhat curious manner: taking the question of proof, she begins, not with a discussion of a book or a traditional paper document, but with an animal, namely, an antelope.

Briet's book starts by stating that Richelet's and Littré's dictionaries define the word "document" in the sense of something used for "instructing or proof." She quotes an unnamed bibliographer as writing, "a document is proof in support of a fact." Briet then quotes the official definition for "document" formulated by the Union Française des Organismes de Documentation: "the total basis for materially fixed knowledge and susceptible of being used for consultation, study, and proof" (7).

Next, passing beyond these definitions, Briet, acknowledges that

> this definition has often been countered by linguists and philosophers, who are necessarily infatuated with minutia and logic. Thanks to their analysis of the content of this idea, one can propose here a definition, which may be, at the present time, the most accurate, but is also the most abstract, and thus, the least accessible: "all concrete or symbolic indexical signs *[indice],* preserved or recorded toward the ends of representing, of reconstituting, or of proving a physical or intellectual phenomenon." (7)

Briet then continues by asking:

> Is a star a document? Is a pebble rolled by a torrent a document? Is a living animal a document? No. But some documents are: the photographs and the catalogs of stars, stones in a museum of mineralogy, and animals that are cataloged and shown in a zoo. (7)

Briet then gives another example of a document: a new kind of antelope is discovered in Africa. The antelope is brought back to France to the

Jardin des Plantes. A press release to newspapers, radio, and newsreels announces its arrival. The discovery "becomes the object of communication in the Academy of Sciences. A professor mentions it in his lecture" (7). The antelope is added to a film track, and it is recorded on a record. When it dies, it is stuffed and preserved in a museum. A monograph appears on it, then it enters a zoological encyclopedia, and then a general encyclopedia. These works are announced, and then they are cataloged in a library. These documents and others are then recopied through drawings, paintings, photographs, film, and microfilms, and then those documents are further selected, analyzed, described, and translated. The end of this trail of evidence is that "their ultimate conservation and utilization are determined by some general techniques and by sound methods for assembling the documents—methods which are studied in national associations and at international Congresses" (8).

Briet ends her introduction with the statement: "The cataloged antelope is an initial document and the other documents are secondary or derived" (8).

Two important events are immediately evident in Briet's text. First is that Briet chooses to talk about documents by beginning with a live animal instead of a paper text (Buckland, "What Is a 'Document'?"). If a live animal is a document, then nonpaper materials such as film, statues, paintings, and the like must have documentary status as well. (Briet does, in fact, name these as constituting secondary forms of documents for the antelope.) With this gesture, Briet effectively breaks the trope of the book as the dominant trope for both documentation and the age of documentation; documentation in the modern age must found its future upon other figures or principles than that of the book.

The second important event in Briet's first few paragraphs of *Qu'est-ce que la documentation?* is that she defines documents by their status as evidence. Evidence, though, can be thought about in different ways. Most commonly, evidence is taken in a positivist sense of being an object or event that is proof for the existence of some factual question. Briet, however, subverts this tendency by appealing to philosophical and linguistic approaches to the problem of evidence, suggesting, in the context of her time, that what seems to be a more semiotic approach is appropriate for thinking about documents as evidence. Central to her argument is the use of the term *"indice"* in the beginning of *Qu'est-ce que la documentation?*, which suggests the importance of defining documents by their indexical relationships to other documents and, moreover, to other documentary representations (such as bibliographical records and metalanguage).

Briet may not have been a semiotician or used the term "semiotics" itself, but she was a librarian influenced by the philosophers and linguists of her day, and every librarian knows the importance of the indexical relations of signs to one another in the placement and definition of bibliographic documents. For example, books can only be cataloged and therefore come into bibliographical existence within the context of previously approved vocabularies, such as subject headings, authority records for authors' names, and approved syntactical structures for subject, name, and even title entries. For a librarian, documents as evidence or facts are established and found by entering into authorized (or as librarians say, "controlled") institutional networks of language. By defining documents within a network or within networks of indexical relations, the documentary object is transformed from being an object per se into a semiotic term within a network of production. And once defined within such a network, it more easily can metaphorically enter other networks, or it can metonymically come to symbolize, and even rhetorically leverage, an existing network.

In addition to Briet's striking assertion that a document or, equally, an evidential fact is such inasmuch as it is defined within institutional and linguistic networks of production, *Qu'est-ce que la documentation?* is significant in that it turns this epistemological model back upon documentation as a profession and thus comes to a sociology of scientific professionalism that is characterized by indexical relationships. Documentation is characterized in Briet's work as an agent within a system of "science," which she identifies as the culture of postwar Western capitalist industrial societies. But inasmuch as documentation symbolizes the method of production within science and yet does so through its own practice, documentation constitutes a metascience of science. What follows from this in Briet's texts is a series of cultural claims for documentation that are based on these metaphorical and metonymical displacements that Briet believes exist between documentation and science. We will later see similar series of displacements in Norbert Wiener's claims for a nascent information science and its relation to what he sees as a culture of science during the late 1940s and 1950s in the United States and Europe. What is important to note here is how a certain privileging of a technical model works to elevate documentation or a science of information socially but at the cost of mapping social space according to the operational values and language of those technical-professional concerns. When the advancement of a professional discourse is brought about through a rhetorical reification of cultural or social space, one has to question the profession's claims to be merely serving a historical or social demand. One must ask the profession what responsibility it assumes in the dissemination of a language that leads to such a reification, and one must ask what types of histories are excluded by this mapping of cultural or social space into the future.

In the following sections in this chapter, I will examine Briet's texts in more detail as to their historical and political implications. First, however, I would like to sketch out Briet's epistemological and sociological model of indexicality more thoroughly by examining a text by Bruno Latour that enacts a striking repetition of Briet's rhetoric and claims for documents and institutional networks in her *Qu'est-ce que la documentation?*

Science and Institutions

Like Briet's example of the recently discovered antelope, Bruno Latour begins his essay on libraries and collections, "Ces réseaux que la raison ignore: laboratoires, bibliothèques, collections," with specimens taken from a distant land. Latour's essay is provocative and, as with Briet's arguments, raises the issue of the semiotic encoding of social space through the presence of master signifiers and technical apparatuses and their social metaphors.

Latour begins his essay with a self-portrait by Pierre Sonnerat in 1776, *Voyage à la Nouvelle-Guinée,* in which Sonnerat is depicted as seated in a tropical environment drawing natural objects while he is surrounded by specimens destined for, among other places, the laboratory and, like Briet's antelope, the Jardin des Plantes.

For Latour, this self-portrait demonstrates several things. First, as in Briet's book, Latour's analysis doesn't focus on books or other paper materials as documents but on natural objects. This is important because Latour argues that information should not be characterized in terms of a representational fact; rather, it is a relation between two places, a periphery and a center (24). This relationship is a practical relationship between what Latour terms a "center of calculation" or "center of measure" *("centre de calcul")* and the objects which that center organizes. What creates the mode of calculus of value for information is institutions, along with signs.

Latour illustrates the sociology of information by telling a story about a bird being brought from the wild and collected within a museum of natural history. Within the museum, the bird is displayed and compared with other birds. What is lost in this act of collecting is the individual in its natural habitat. What is gained is the ability to compare the individual with other known species and thus to categorize it within an existing species or to identify and position it as an individual of a new species within a series of known orders or indexes (such as within the discourses of taxonomy, morphology, or genetics, as well as through practices of display and preservation and the institutional life of the museum and certain professions). Consequently, this universalizing of the individual into a species then allows certain types of institutional management based on principles of ecological conservation, eradication, and so on. For Latour, the action of defining the individual within universal discursive and institutional orders and systems then allows for a return to the individual in terms of knowledge; this return is part of a process of scientific verification.

For Latour, the networked and indexical naming of objects in their collection involves a distribution and redistribution of objects along lines of the properties and values that function through a *centre de calcul.* In this way, libraries, documentation centers, and museums invest and redistribute properties to their artifacts in an analogical manner to capitalization (39). Like a map that allows various elements of a space to be compared, the introduction of a group of standards allows named differences to formally appear and named constants to appear as content. Even though a *centre de calcul* establishes a broad band of common measure, Latour argues that within this measure there remain different series across which an object must be translated. Thus, the "real" for Latour appears not through representation alone but through the constants that remain across these differences. *Centres de calcul* point to the real through a "veil of documents" and discourses (as Briet writes, quoting the philosopher Raymond Bayer in *Qu'est-ce que la documentation?* [7]), and Latour suggests that we argue about that real based upon the constants that remain through that veil of documents and discourses.

The upshot of Latour's argument is that libraries are not just collecting institutions devoted to preservation, nor do they simply offer perspectives on the world, but instead, as institutions, they constitute a manner of establishing proof and the criteria for proof. Like Briet, by appealing to scientific discourse and to institutional and semiotic networks, Latour makes socially dynamic the functions of canon formation and preservation that libraries serve for the human sciences.[6] His goal is to show libraries and their collections not so much as constitutive of culture but as dynamic agencies in the scientific production of the real.

Latour's argument positions libraries within institutional and scientific networks of information production, just as Briet positions documentalists and documentation centers as dynamic agents of information production in our "scientific" culture. What is striking here is that despite a forty-five-year difference, and despite a lack of evidence for any direct influence between Briet and Latour (Briet's work remains relatively unknown in contemporary France), both of their narratives not only have similar goals for repositioning the meaning of those institutions called "libraries" toward scientific production but also, remarkably, utilize an almost identical rhetorical strategy, beginning with the substitution of biological materials for bibliographical materials. By setting up this primary substitution, traditional bibliographical material is brought within a system of production that is named as "scientific." And as such, the metonymical play between "scientific production" and the work done in the service of "science" takes place in Latour's work as it does in Briet's.

Latour's notion of the *centre de calcul,* of course, attempts to account for this metonymical play between production and product by locating both the method of work and the organizational institution for that work within the cultural institutions of science. What it fails to account for, as in Briet's work, however, are the social processes of production through which "science" becomes the master signifier for both the logic of information production and for the product and value of information. This is to say that it fails to account for this production and product as a conceptual apparatus within culture at large on the one hand and as an organizing narrative for Latour's own sociology on the other hand. Most problematic from the aspect of what I will next discuss, Latour's work and Briet's work refuse to examine the term "science" as a trope for institutionally governed social practices or, further, as a term in metaphorical equivalence with "information." There is no account in either of their works of why we should think of documents in terms of science, of information as being scientific or factual, or of knowledge in terms of indexical notions of evidence, proof, or fact. Knowledge in terms of indexicality and in terms of a calculus of value are simply assumed, and this assumption is validated through the institutional functions attributed to science, even though the term "science" is merely a trope for that very indexicality and calculus of value within the practice of certain social institutions and certain discursive orders.

In other words, both authors fail to account for the production of "science" or of "information" in terms of social production and instead are content with describing these terms and their functions as cultural logics. Both Latour's and Briet's "sociologies" or descriptive narratives of production merely reproduce an ideological order rather than critically examine it. For Briet, the reason for this failure lies in the "practical" necessity that the profession of documentation, *as a profession,* must serve the "necessity of our time," which she sees as "scientific" production in a "scientific" culture. This notion of "practice" in Briet (even in Briet's "theoretical" writings) means that documentation must both methodologically mimic science and also produce scientific products for use within a scientific production of culture. Professional practice, therefore, should follow the ideological trope of science both in order to serve its demand and to advance the profession within the cultural domains that are governed by that ideology (here, not only scientific institutions but culture or society in general as "science"). Since professions gain their power by seeming to serve culture or society at large, however, it behooves the profession to advance the dominant ideology throughout culture or society in order to advance its own status. Thus, as will be shown in the next chapter in the discussion of Norbert Wiener's work, at a social or cultural level, the work of a science of information becomes difficult to distinguish from the work of rhetorically and historically constructing a culture of information to match a conception and ideology of knowledge as information and to match the information and communication technologies that are constructed around such a conception and ideology. Serving the ideological trope of science and its technologies, as well as the needs of a corresponding information profession, becomes a matter of organizing cultural and social needs around this trope. As I have suggested, part of this historical task requires the deployment of a rhetoric that attempts to naturalize social space around certain conceptions of science and around certain techniques and technologies. Professions attempt to leverage history by means of language in order to create opportunities for themselves.

Organizing the Cultural Needs of "Science"

In the context of the cultural and historical demands of "science" upon documentation, Briet's statement that "the organization of documentation is a technique of our time" ("Bibliothécaires" 43) may be read not only in terms of the demands of the practice and institutions of science upon the actual organization of specific documents but also in terms of a culture of science's demands upon the institutional "organization" of documentation itself. Though Briet's phrase is ambiguous, Briet's work as a whole argues that science as a cultural paradigm forced into existence the institution of documentation as well as its techniques of organizing documents. If Briet's claim is true, then her texts themselves must be examined as reactions to the ideological imperatives of a culture of science and must be critiqued in terms of their collaboration, resistance, or critical distance to these imperatives. In fact, as we will see for Briet, documentation must work together with science in order to co-produce the future. Any distance that the profession has from science is only to serve to advance science. Thus, in Briet's work, the dialectic between professions and general culture is not one of opposition but rather one of constructing an ideology from the material and linguistic resources that a professional organization can muster. In truth, of course, science as Briet will describe it doesn't actually exist. Its cultural nature is that of ideology, and it is documentation, along with other institutions, that sets itself the task of extending that ideology and further hegemonizing culture in terms of a language of documentation and information.

For Briet, science is made up of professional organizations, tools, and, foremost, techniques and technologies. In *Qu'est-ce que la documentation?*, Briet locates the beginnings of documentation in the late nineteenth century, a period that witnessed a massive expansion of printed and typed documentary forms (9). For Briet, technological and organizational developments in society necessitate a corresponding development in documentary technique, both in order to respond to the subsequent flood of documents and to serve further social developments. In *Qu'est-ce que la documentation?*, Briet argues that industrial progress demands not only better access to scientific documents but also cultural developments that prepare for and support such progress. Documentation performs both these roles as a science in the service of science.

Briet's texts do very little to critically discriminate "science" from industrial progress, and her examples of industrial or scientific progress are those of Western capitalist countries. Further, her texts explicitly characterize such progress in terms of the development of a global culture, thus demanding that documentation be spread to the "countless masses" according to the doctrine of postwar "cultural assistance" or "development" (45). Briet's texts describe documentary technique in terms of modernist industrial production—that is, according to the tropes of dynamism, rapidity, precision, efficiency, and standardization. Such terms move back and forth between a vocabulary of professional technique and of cultural description, and it is by means of this weaving that an ideology of an industrial society governed by information is created.

Briet recognizes that a cultural crisis involving overproduction has occurred in modernity, but like Otlet, she sees documentary technique as a way of managing this crisis. For Briet, the overproduction of documentary materials is a natural event predicated on the advancement of science. Briet's "professional" interests allow her to see documentation only as a current and future technique for dealing with information fragmentation and overproduction in culture rather than seeing documentation itself as a symptom of modernist production and politics at the level of language. Issues such as media saturation and the commoditization of language through information and communication technologies would not occur to her as a professional because they would then involve issues of ideology and politics toward which the professional must remain neutral. In Briet's "Bibliothécaires et documentalistes," Briet approvingly cites her colleague Robert Pagès in placing documentation within the service of what she identifies as "culture":

> It is necessary to return to Pagès.[7] His message has not had, at the moment or when he made his statements, all the discussion that it merited, because it lacked an audience prepared to receive it. This is why, two years later, we attempted to explain those things which in our eyes were documentation: a technique of intellectual work, a new profession, a need of our *time*. Pagès' dialectics and axioms are irrefutable. They may be summarized through some phrases pulled from his text and placed end to end: the crisis of definition which we suffer from is only a symptom of an organizational crisis and a division of cultural work; an inevitable industrialization of intellectual work has produced the machinery (organizations and tools) that make the evolution of a new cultural technique necessary, a technique which will soon be socially decisive. Documentation is a segment of culture, but it includes the domain of librarians: the librarian is a particular case of the documentalist—both are distributors of culture. The duties of the librarian, in fact, aren't fulfilled until she learns general documentary technique. (44)

As an "information professional," Briet's concerns are not involved with critically exploring the historical and political agency of her profession beyond those that are dictated by socially or technically defined tasks. By default, then, professional agency becomes synonymous with ideological advancement, even if, at times, it serves as the liberal counterpoint to a conservative politics. In this, Briet is totally "professional" in the manner that Dewey and Otlet were: her work is not critical but rather is productive and exploitative of the dominant cultural tropes for science. For Briet, to be socially successful, the profession of documentation needs to define itself indexically within the ideology of science as well as then attempt to promote itself as the science that leads science. In other words, it needs to define itself within an ideological horizon and then define itself *as* that horizon. In Briet's work, this is performed first by the metaphorical identification of documentation or information with science and then by the characterization of the present as a scientific age that is led by information. In Briet's texts, the rhetorical tropes of metaphor and metonymy have very definite political and historical roles for constructing culture in general and for positioning documentation within politics and history.

In characterizing documentation as "dynamic" within a system of technical and institutional relations, Briet, in part, continues the tradition of "library economy" that Dewey established at the Columbia School of Library Economy in 1887.[8] For Briet, documentary science, however, is less involved with the traditional European library's emphasis upon collection and canonical hermeneutics but is more interested in user services and in exchanging information materials within economies of cultural production. The documentalist not only must be deeply involved in the exchange of materials within "scientific" cultural production but also must lead the individual scientist, indeed, as Briet states, "like the dog on the hunt—totally before [the researcher], guided, guiding" ("Bibliothécaires 43). This demand requires that the documentalist inhabit the process of science, even as he or she stays ahead of it ("the organizations and tools of documentation work in the immediate, in the becoming *[le devenir]* of science" [42]).

Documentation emulates science in terms of its being "dynamic," and this dynamism involves a rapidity and precision in information gathering and use that matches what Briet understands as science's demand for time-sensitive materials and for precise information (42). Documentation networks documentary and human agents together in an energetic system of industrial-cultural production. Echoing Otlet's conception of the book as a technical organism within a living intellectual economy, Briet writes that "the dynamism of living documentation joins with the dynamism of the mind in its quest for truth" (*Qu'est-ce que la documentation?* 44). Further, this living dynamism corresponds to a shift in cultural experiences of space and time that occurs with the interjection of information and communication technologies into everyday lives and research: "[For] the telephone, the microfilm reader, the typewriter, the dictaphone and the telescript give to intellectual effort a *different rhythm*" (11). (I should note here that in chapter 5, I discuss this problem of industrial rhythm through Walter Benjamin's work, though in terms of "shock.") Intellectual activity and "the mind" for Briet have been changed through the social mediation of information and communication technologies. Briet's writings solidly locate human subjectivity, at least in terms of intellectual activity, within what Paul N. Edwards has termed a "cyborg discourse" (2).

Briet quotes with approval a statement by Robert Pagès that "documentation is to culture what the machine is to industry" (*Qu'est-ce que la documentation?* 13–14), a statement that proposes an analogy not only between human agency and machine agency, technique and technology, but also between modernist cultural production and industrial production. Now, the rhetoric of analogy proposes standardization, and in systems theory, standards lead to systems. Cultural production and industrial production, intellectual labor and technological work, are thus joined in *Qu'est-ce que la documentation?* under the trope of science or, simply, intelligence, terms that turn analogies into natural explanations for technical-technological interactions and that introduce the possibility of smoothly operating cybernetic systems. The "omnipresence of intelligence," for Briet, connects the work of the body and the mind, the tool and the brain: "The hand has served the mind; the tool has developed the brain. The mind, in return, guides the hand. Such is the omnipresence of intelligence" (13). It is precisely this "omnipresence of intelligence" that will be called in cybernetics "information" and that will join technological production and culture, technical information transfer and language, in a "scientific" model of personal identity and social community. For Briet, "the progress in cybernetics, especially at the Massachusetts Institute of Technology," only foreshadows the "need for documentary man to become prepared to command, with all his faculties alert, the robots of tomorrow" (29). As discussed in chapter 3, the trope of "man" is called in to "humanly" explain and rationalize the "cultural necessity" of human-technological systems as well as to balance a science-fiction anxiety about technological systems escaping the "mind" of man.

Not surprisingly, as the first chapter of *Qu'est-ce que la documentation?* closes, Briet's argument for a systemic relation between human technique and mechanical technology takes a further step into the future. For Briet, the analogical and systemic relationships between human technique and technology that support her cultural claims for documentation open up to a "new humanism" based on these relationships. Documentation, as a sign of the present and as a harbinger of the future, not only responds to this "new humanism" but also prepares the ground for this new humanism in terms of its "technique." At the heart of this technique is "the coordination" of diverse "sectors in the same organization." Briet reads the preparation of future culture and society in terms of those techniques of selection, combination, and standardization that lie at the heart of bibliographic control. Documentation both mimics the present and models the future, not only in terms of its own theoretical characterizations but also in terms of its own practice, and it can do this because it is, essentially, "scientific." As a "scientific" professional discourse at the service of "culture," documentation is justly both descriptive and prescriptive of social norms in its theory and its practice. The documentalist cannot abdicate this social responsibility toward the "new humanism":

> It is not too much to speak of a new *humanism* in this regard. A different breed of researcher "is in the making" [English in original]. It springs from the reconciliation of the machine and the mind *[l'esprit]*. Modern man may not repudiate any aspect of his heritage. Supported by the rich experiences of the past which have been passed on to him, he resolutely turns toward the world of tomorrow. The constant development *[devenir]* of humanity requires that the masses and the individual adapt. Here, technology *[la technique]* is the symptom of a social need. "One characteristic of modern documentation is that of the coordination" of diverse "sectors in the same organization." (14)

The Same Organization

If both the "masses and the individual"—as well as librarians and other information workers and scholars—need to adapt to this "new humanism" of industrial cyborg organization led by industry, then how are they to do it?

For Briet, there are two ways that the "masses and the individual" become "the future": first, technical standardization, and second, education. Standardization is the type of precision most favored by the dynamics of global production, for by bringing materials onto a plane of standard consistency (as demonstrated by Latour's concept of the *centre de calcul*), different elements may enter into operational relationships with one another, thus forming a system of production. "Standardization" for Briet means, first of all, not only bibliographical standards but also larger sets of standards for communication, beginning with the "problem" of language's semantic variances.

Language is a particularly important and sticky area in Briet's advocacy of global standardization for the purpose of scientific development, and as such it nicely illuminates the point that standardization is not simply a technical issue in documentation but also a cultural one. On the one hand, Briet recognizes that "there is nothing more important, nor more rare, than recognizing cultural specialization and the ability of being a polyglot" (*Qu'est-ce que la documentation?* 25). On the other hand, "the principal obstacle to unification remains the multiplicity of languages, of this Babel which stands in opposition to both understanding and to cooperation" (43). With the failure of Esperanto, Briet argues, one wouldn't dare to invent a universal language. Thankfully, however, "the major languages, that is to say, English, French, and Spanish, tend to spread and to become the indispensable interpreters of civilized people" (43). German, Briet writes, has "retreated," Russian is no longer in the forefront, and "the Orientals always speak their language and another language" anyway (43). Thus, linguistic standardization for documentation across the globe emerges in terms of a postwar security council of languages belonging to former major European colonial empires and the subsequent dominant capitalist allied countries.

Science and information's progress (which, in Briet's work, is always bound together with the advancement of capitalist industries) needs the standardization of education and language in order to proceed. This leads to a number of "developmental" steps in order for science to take root in the third world. "Standardization" occurs in a number of steps, leading from linguistic and educational standardization to documentary and communicational standardization and finally to industrial standardization, so that third-world countries may be "developed" to the "scientific" level of first-world countries through this process. The cultural standards and languages of Euro-American capitalist countries level and then prepare the cultural ground for documentary processes, and documentary processes then allow industry to flourish. Documentation is, thus, part of the rational leveling and reorganization of national and ethnic cultures that mark the "progress" of postwar capitalist industries and is part of the battle against other forms of social organization—both traditional and communist—that threaten it.[9] For Briet, standardization is more than a major trope in the language of technology. Within the culture of "science" on the scale of "the global," standardization is an integral part of global cultural production. Documentation, which is always first concerned with standardization and linkage, is therefore not only a vehicle for science but also an exemplary symbol of science and the scientific age in modernity.

In the drive to globalize the world via the forces of technical standardization, cultural standardization, and information science and technology, education plays a special role for Briet, both domestically and in foreign policy. Specialized education, Briet repeats again and again throughout her writings, is what separates librarians from documentalists, the cultured from the uncultured, and the developing world from the undeveloped world. "Scientific" education is specific in terms of its subject fields and universal in terms of its desire for global application. The properly trained documentalist is a symbol of this modern form of education as well as a leading player within it.

Briet accepts without hesitation the modernist argument for progress, namely, that "humanity tends toward unification." Within this historical tendency toward global unification, documentalists have the special role, in conjunction with UNESCO's Library Division, of being "new types of missionaries" and "initiating into culture the more or less uncultured masses and of increasing their contact with scientists *[avec les savants]*" (*Qu'est-ce que la documentation?* 41). For Briet, "the battle against illiteracy, the organization of a reading public, biblioeconomy, and documentation in all its forms, comes in the wake of the driving force of the exploration vessel flying the United Nations flag" (41). UNESCO and documentation are the explorers and missionaries for modernity within the guise of development specialists acting according to the mandates of science and information technique and technology.

Otlet, Briet, and Beyond

Today, Otlet's and Briet's rhetoric and arguments continue in government and industry announcements that information and communication technologies lead to global economic, social, and cultural development as well as to international understanding; that a universal network of information standards leads to "bringing the world together" in an age of dynamic and flexible production; and that information and communication technologies in the "information age" will lead to greater international justice, peace, and community. For Otlet and Briet and for their fellow documentalists who made such an international ruckus in the library world before and just after World War II, documentation quite obviously was a *cultural* event that had definite political goals and effects, including shaping the future—and the possibility for a future—in a particular way. As seen from the rhetoric of their texts, this task of shaping the future was intrinsic to their writings. By the documentalists' own arguments, their professional discourse as information scientists must be understood and judged at a *cultural* level, before and beyond its status as a strictly professional or technical discourse. Along with a lack of reliance upon (but not an absence of) mathematical and statistical formulation and research, this characteristic most distinguishes their work from that of information science proper during and after World War II.

Information science during and after World War II defined itself more thoroughly through quantitative research and formal methods than before, and thus, at both a rhetorical and institutional level, it fulfilled the desires of the documentalists to be more "scientific" according to the dominant cultural understandings of the sciences of the time. Sadly, the historical forgetting of documentation is probably a function of the greater emphasis upon quantitative research during and after World War II, as quantitative research became a dominant cultural paradigm for "science" during and after the war years, in particular as the quantitative social sciences merged with engineering in such new areas as cybernetics. Ironically, as quantitative methods became more culturally important, so the self-acknowledgment of the importance of culture in research became less important in comparison to its claims toward operational efficiency. In a sense, the historical importance of documentation has been a victim of its own rhetoric. This is unfortunate, however, because this historical abandon further masks the important role that professional and authoritative texts and institutions have in defining a broad culture in terms of narrow professional and technical interests and through understandings and rhetorics of "science" that are beholden to economic dominants and political ideologies.

The next chapter examines the popular dissemination of information theory through the writings of Warren Weaver and Norbert Wiener and the rhetorical strategies they employed in order to apply quantitative and operational theories of information to general culture and society. Whereas the documentalists' writings demonstrate an attempt to bring culture within the domain of a technical-technological notion of information science, Weaver's and Wiener's writings already assume that culture is but one element in statistically measurable information transfer and the science thereof. This appropriation of culture and, with it, language to a quantitatively defined notion of information may be seen as the complete appropriation of textual and social hermeneutics to an ideology of information. The operationalization of culture and language within the very site of texts and reading marks the closure of any tensions that might exist between material documents and ideal notions of informational fact. In order to deconstruct this closure and reopen textual and social hermeneutics, and thus in order to de-operationalize and de-quantify notions of culture within an ideology of information, it will be necessary to show

how Wiener's and Weaver's own texts remain unwieldy and highly literary in the midst of their rational and scientific claims and how their social claims for "scientific" information theory are haunted through and through by cultural and political ideologies.

3 ■ Information Theory, Cybernetics, and the Discourse of "Man"

Wherever you go, a new
           combination
    and upon its liquid, language
depends. In a true tongue, what passes the throat is thought
and those who sing don't follow time.
         They make it

                      —Jean Day, "Strait of Fascination"

In order to understand the history and philosophy of information in the twentieth century, it is necessary to understand the intermixing of a variety of historical streams into a discourse on "information." As I have suggested in the preceding chapter, one stream is the tradition of European documentation that sees material documents as information because of the indexical placement of such materials within discursive and institutional systems. Another important stream for comprehending our current understanding of information is the communications model for information, which sees information according to what Michael J. Reddy has called the "conduit metaphor" for communication. According to this model or metaphor, information is the flow and exchange of a message, originating from one speaker, mind, or source and received by another. Analogous to theories of production and exchange in liberal capitalism, information, here, is understood as created by the "free" will of one person and is then transferred through the "medium" or market of public language into the ear and mind of another person, at which point the second person acknowledges the correct value of the original intention by his or her performative actions. Implicit in this standard model for communication and information are such notions as the intentionality of the speaker, the self-evident "presence" of that intention in his or her words, a set of hearers or "users" who receive the information and who demonstrate the correctness of that reception in action or use, and the freedom of choice in regard to the speaker's ability to say one thing rather than another, as well as even the receiver's freedom to choose to receive one message rather than another in the marketplace of ideas.

Each of these streams is important to the social dissemination and application of information theory and cybernetics, beginning in the Cold War and proceeding to today. Beginning with military research in the areas of servomechanism command and control, as well as in the areas of telecommunication, cryptography, probability theory, and game theory, information was characterized along lines of the conduit metaphor as this metaphor shuttled between, and collapsed the differences between, technical applications and models and social applications and models. Through such events as the Josiah Macy Jr. cybernetics conferences in the late 1940s and early 1950s and the Macy Foundation conference on "panic" in 1958, information theory and cybernetics expanded from a technical application to become a general theory for personal psychology and social community.[1] Information theory and cybernetics were so successful in this expansion because the conduit metaphor already had a solid basis in popular understandings of language. Today, of course, information theory and cybernetics, as well as systems theory, remain solidly in evidence in organizational analyses and in second-order cybernetics. Central to these approaches is the need to functionally define component parts of events and to operationally understand events in terms of representational systems that then can be used for management. Taking a positivist course directly opposed to earlier romantic and modernist conceptualizations of meaning based on the sublime and the unconscious, as well as largely ignoring work in structuralist and formalist approaches to language on the European continent, the primary assumption of communication and information theory after World War II, especially in the United Kingdom and the United States, has been the possibility of probabilistic descriptions of phenomena for the "successful" explanation and management of uncertain environments.[2] Consequently, the concept of "information" has come to be thought of as quantitatively measurable and thus "factual."

The canonical book of information theory is Claude E. Shannon and Warren Weaver's *The Mathematical Theory of Communication* (1949). This book contains two papers: Shannon's original paper ("The Mathematical Theory of Communication"), which is an explication of information theory in technical systems, and Weaver's explanation of Shannon's paper

("Recent Contributions to the Mathematical Theory of Communication"), which expands that paper's technical theory to larger social spaces.[3]

In this chapter, I examine how Warren Weaver and Norbert Wiener, the father of cybernetics, socially expanded the technical theory of information and thus contributed to the particular type of "information age" we live in today. One cannot help but discover in their writings a general theory of "man" based on the conduit model of communication that—though it has been extended throughout biology (particularly through sociobiology)[4] and does not seem at first glance to be traditional humanism—nonetheless inscribes "man" and many other creatures and society as a whole in a communicational model attributed to, as Wiener claimed, what is most "human" in "human beings." Consequently, I end this chapter by critically engaging this claim and by proposing a sense of information and community contrary to this humanism, not in order to arrive at an even more general theory of communication, being, identity, or community, but precisely in order to subvert all attempts to arrive at a general theory. Instead of a general theory of human, and even animal, communication, I propose through the work of other theorists a notion of information that stresses the site-specific and temporal nature of *affects* rather than the communicational *effects* of messages. In this manner, I hope to engage information theory at its site of historical production, to critique its social metaphors, and to propose a sense of information based on events and affects that resist representation and management.

One of the consequences of such a critique of information theory would be that the classical subject of "man," which is the agency of production and reception in the social extension of information theory, is severely brought into doubt in terms of its ontological reality. Inasmuch as this chapter performs this project, one might say that it belongs to a type of "deconstruction" of information theory and a questioning of its traditional notions of meaning and intentional agency—for example, informational "facts," creators, producers, and users, as well as an understanding of language based on "communication" (that is, upon language as representation). Thus, this chapter opens a critique of the Anglo-American positive social science traditions of information and communication by shedding light on the history and logic of some of the central texts on information theory and social context after World War II. In this chapter, some dangers involved in a global extension of the conduit metaphor and notions of linguistic command and control are discussed, and I show how deeply humanistic and reactionary such a past, current, and future "information age" may be.

The General Theory of Communication

In "Recent Contributions to the Mathematical Theory of Communication," Weaver begins by arguing for a general, "broad" theory of communication, defined in terms of how "one mind may affect another" in a context that "would include the procedures by means of which one mechanism affects another mechanism." Weaver further proposes that such a general theory of communication would be applicable not only to human speech and writing and to machine affects but also to "music of any sort, and to still or moving pictures, as in television" and "to the pictorial arts, the theatre, the ballet, and in fact all human behavior" (Shannon and Weaver 3–4).

According to Weaver, a broad theory of communication as affect covers three "levels": the first level is the technical problem involving the electronic transmission of signals; the second level is the semantic problem ("How precisely do the transmitted symbols convey the desired meaning?"); and the third level is "the effectiveness problem" ("How effectively does the received meaning affect conduct in the desired way?") (4). Further, Weaver states that the second and third levels may, "to a significant degree," be subsumed in the first level (6). From these initial points, we can see that Weaver's general theory of communication attempts to inscribe all affective signs and relations into (1) the original or subjective intention of a message, (2) the transmission of a message across a neutral and clear medium, and (3) the re-presentation of the intention of the message in its reception (and its correctness measured in terms of behavioral effects). Further, by this last gesture, Weaver suggests that an informational reading of sensory, emotive, or cognitive affect reduces all affective events to being *effective* events (thus requiring an intentional or causal subject-object relationship and introducing issues of probability, measurement, noise and delay, and feedback).

Weaver sketches out the conduit model for communication in a drawing that is a reproduction of the one printed in Shannon's original paper (see the following figure). In Weaver's text, what is conveyed by this diagram is that a message originates from a source, enters a transmission device, and then is transmitted as a signal across a medium. During this transmission, the signal encounters various degrees of nonrelevant "noise" from a third source or from the environment in general. Having passed through the "noise," the message is then received as a signal and is interpreted as the intended message through the correct behavior of a receiving agency at the destination point.

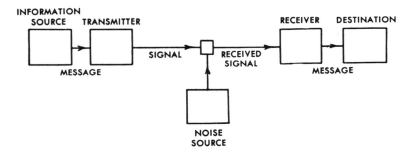

Weaver gives to the reader a set of examples for this process of communication or information: telegraphy, telephony, radio transmission, and the oral communication of one speaker in the presence of another. The presence of this last example within a set of technological examples is no accident: the diagram originates in the conduit metaphor for language as communication,[5] and its power is then reinforced by an appeal to "scientific" or technological devices for communication. As Weaver explains, "In oral speech, the information source is the brain, [and] the transmitter is the voice mechanism producing the varying sound pressure (the signal) which is transmitted through the air (the channel)" (7). What is carried by means of the voice, of course, are ideas that are then transmitted to another brain by means of the ear of the hearer. Spoken or written languages are transmitters of ideas, Weaver reasons, and since such languages can be, in some sense, measured (by sound waves and the like), their information content should be measurable as well.

Despite already interpreting Shannon's technical theory in terms of a common model for human language, Weaver argues that the notion of "information" in his general theory "must not be confused with its ordinary usage" (8). A unit of information is the amount of "freedom of choice" an agency has between what can be sent and what is sent. Information is a probabilistic calculation between what can be sent and what is sent, between the probable total information of a system and a choice to make use of one portion of it rather than another. Inversely, reception is a function of statistical redundancy: the more statistically redundant a message is within a system, the greater the likelihood that it will be successfully received and understood. In his two major books on the topic,

Cybernetics and *The Human Use of Human Beings,* Norbert Wiener also characterizes information in terms of "freedom of choice" in order to create a liberal appeal for "freedom of speech" and "freedom of information" in the context of U.S. politics during the Cold War.

The question remains, however, what is the result of reducing the value and meaning of information to a calculus and system based on probability and statistical measure? Especially by explicitly inscribing the arts within such criteria for informational value, Weaver effectively cancels out critical and formalist critiques of representation and representational systems and thus reduces all anomalies or alterities of representation to "abnormal" statistical appearances within the range of a normative communication system. And by reducing all affect to this theoretical model, Weaver reduces the value and meaning of language, societies, and communities to operational criteria. We must remember that the "freedom of choice" in sending (and receiving) messages, here, means a *statistical* choice. Consequently, we should remember that Weaver's (and Wiener's) model is based on a formally complete representation of affects (in terms of effects) and behavior. "Freedom" is an operational measure of what degrees of agency are statistically possible given a standard range and measure of affects.

For Weaver, the notion of statistical uncertainty (or equally, "freedom" or "information") in a communications system has "either good or bad connotations." The "good" connotation of information is, of course, the freedom of the sender; this is a "desirable" uncertainty. On the other hand, "uncertainty which arises because of errors or because of the influence of noise is undesirable uncertainty" (Shannon and Weaver 19). Weaver here conflates "freedom" in the sense of classical subjectivity and liberal political theory with a sense of "freedom" based on statistical measure within closed systems. It is through this rhetorical conflation of subjective agency with that of statistical possibility that technical and social regimes are merged in a normative and operational model of society and that "information" becomes equated with both subjective freedom and with systemic possibility.

Weaver's model, as a general model of affect as communication and information, contrasts a statistical system against the background and intrusion of an environment filled with irrelevant "noise." Like Norbert Wiener's view of nature as a dangerous and chaotic uncertainty, Weaver's communicational system must attempt to screen out or "translate" noise into terms that the system can understand and control. This division between system and environment (to borrow Luhmann's terms) must, however, be understood as an effect of the conduit model itself, for the problem with "noise" is that it disrupts the statistical distribution of the system and it confuses the acts of intention and reception. If noise were allowed to freely invade the system, freedom of choice, intention, and a correctness of re-presentation in reception would be impossible to determine accurately. System and intentional agency would give way to chaos and confusion.

Of course we must ask, if "noise" were not logically premised as an intrusion, how would we know that a system was a system and, consequently, that a reception came from an intention? As an intrusion, noise simultaneously breaches the boundary of a system and marks that set of relations as a system. If it were not for the assumption of noise, there would be no system, nor would reception have anything to measure intention against. To put this another way, if there were neither bad information nor good information, neither bad uncertainty nor good uncertainty, but rather uncertain uncertainty, how could a system of information exist, especially one with intentional speakers and listeners? The existence of both a communication or information system and that of an intentional self-identity to the "original" message depends upon a logical exteriority rather than upon the empirical fact of noise, or further, of system or intention.

"Noise" is not an "empirical fact" but rather a logically necessary component for the existence of Weaver and Wiener's information theory. Further, behind the division of good noise (good uncertainty) and bad noise (bad uncertainty) lies an even more frightening noise for Weaver and Wiener—a noise of the uncertainty of the division between good and bad noise (that is to say, good or bad information). And this uncertainty is what the division between an intentional and positivist system and noise both suppresses and expresses. Noise, in fact, allows the system to exist as a unitary and conscious system. Together, noise and system mask that even more frightful "other," namely, that uncertain uncertainty that may be either communication or noise, system or environment.

Against such chaos, language, behavioral affects, persons, and communities—as operational systems and as systems within systems—are problematics for theoretical description and for practical design by communication and information theory. As Weaver writes:

> Language must be designed (or developed) with a view
> to the totality of things that man may wish to say; but
> not being able to accomplish everything, it too should
> do as well as possible as often as possible. That is to say,
> it too should deal with its task, statistically. (27)

This design of language assumes a knowledge of all that it is possible to say. It assumes, to use Wittgenstein's metaphor of sight for language, that we can see beyond the limits of our vision. Indeed, this is the task of a complete description of communication—to see beyond communication. It is the purpose of information theory—as a theory of design or engineering—to create the conditions for the proper transmission of meaning, assuming, of course, that such a mechanism can recognize what man "may wish to say."

And the trick here, of course, is to be able to describe such *wishes* or desires—an infinite and deeply problematic task from the point of view of, say, the unconscious. Of course, the positivist assumptions of information theory do not proceed from such a psychoanalytic viewpoint and in fact would treat the notion of unconscious utterances like any other uncertainty, that is, as noise. But the failure to address such a notion as the unconscious (which symbolizes an excess of meaning to language and an uncontrollability of vocabulary) points to the very failure of a metaphor based on a technical model to address social space and history.

Classical information theory fails to account for nonrepresentational affects of communication or language, and this can be seen in Weaver's appropriation of what he identifies as the semantic and affective aspects of information by the technical aspect of signal transmission. The model of communication and language that information theory and cybernetics follows leads only to operational theories wherein wishes are what are statistically possible. Thus, in the name of rational structures of communication and "factual" information, desire is channeled through imagined statistical control over words and things.

The role of information theory, and its theoreticians and designers, is to give possibilities that are proper to an imagined standard of "man":

> An engineering communication theory is just like a very proper and discreet girl accepting your telegram. She pays no attention to the meaning, whether it be sad or joyous, or embarrassing. But she must be prepared to deal with all that come to her desk. This idea that a communication system ought to try to deal with all possible messages, and that the intelligent way to try is to base design on the statistical character of the source, is surely not without significance for communication in general. Language must be designed (or developed) with a view to the totality of things that man may wish to say. . . . (Shannon and Weaver 27)

Weaver's reading of Shannon's text involves a generalization of a technical theory of information or communication from a technical to a social and linguistic model. Human beings, language, and community, here, are those organisms and systems that are not chaotic, are not noise. The question, however, is whether such a theory is descriptive of real events or is itself symptomatic of an attempt to construct such beings and systems. Is information theory—as a general theory of communication— descriptive or prescriptive? As a "scientific" theory of communication, Weaver, of course, believes his general theory to be descriptive, but inasmuch as Weaver and Wiener claim that information theory is an obedient servant to that which is "proper" to man, they beg the question of how much such a theory itself attempts to create and recreate those conditions for the appearance of "man." The concept of "man" is characterized in their texts by a freedom of choice equivalent to bondage: man's freedom of choice is given by the "scientific" system that claims to serve man, to hold man, and to allow man to speak.

Weaver's generalization of information theory to human agency and community obliterates language and being's historicity and reduces agency and affects to operational functions within designed social systems. The propriety that information claims to give to man is that which is proposed through a logic of identity and exclusion, attempting to describe man's possibilities in language through a language of design and normative statistics. What is left of information are not the affects of the human nor the affects of any other beings in the universe but rather the effects of design, command, and control. By means of a binary logic of system and noise, beings, their languages, and their affects lose their own specificity and creative temporality. Their freedom is not that of creating time and social space from their affective relations; rather, their freedom is granted to them in terms of statistical measures and norms. The task of information theory and cybernetics to prescribe social space by the theory of information or communication aims toward representing beings, language, and communication in terms of operational relations.

As we will see, in order to accomplish this ordering of "man" and "nature," the authority of "the scientist" is necessary. The vanguard task of the scientist for Norbert Wiener is to ensure that information theory remains central to the description and functions of society so that the message of man's being as that of *scientific information and communication* remains constantly sent throughout society.

The First Law, the Law of the Law, the Law of Translation

> The first law of the law, whatever the second or third one is, is to know what it wants.
>
> —Norbert Wiener, *The **Human** Use of Human Beings*

As Wiener's quote makes clear within the context of his emphasis upon the "Human" in the title to the 1950 edition of his work, the clarity of the law is an imperative for that being which is called "man." Indeed, clarity in communication is so important to Wiener's conception of human communication that the dedication of his book in both the 1950 and 1954 editions rather personally expresses the problematic of representation or reproduction that leads to such a demand. For the problematic of reproduction lies at the heart of any comparative study of linguistics, as well as any act of human generation:

> To the memory of my father
> Leo Wiener
> formerly Professor of Slavic languages
> at Harvard University
> my closest mentor and dearest antagonist

Inasmuch as Wiener's book attempts to clarify and solve the ambiguity of familiarity and antagonism that Wiener feels toward the problematic of (linguistic) reproduction, Wiener sees his book as confronting both the menace of censorship in Cold War United States and the totalitarianism of Soviet communist society. For Wiener, "free" communication and information are what are at stake in transmission. In his writings of the Cold War period, Wiener never hesitates to evoke the liberal doctrine that democracy and truth are tied to free, unambiguous communication and information. As Wiener expresses in regard to the issue of civil justice, "as in the case of contracts, unambiguity, precedent, and a good clear tradition of interpretation are worth more than a theoretical equity, particularly in the assessment of responsibilities" (1950, 115). Language, for Wiener, is a social contract between speakers that demands a Cartesian "clarity" so that transmission and reproduction are possible. These rules for language apply to the State's "speech" as well:

> It is the first duty of the law to see that the obligations
> and rights given to an individual in a certain stated situ-
> ation are unambiguous. Moreover, there should be a

> body of legal interpretation which is as far as possible in-
> dependent of the will and the interpretation of the par-
> ticular authorities consulted. Reproducibility is prior to
> equity, for without it there can be no equity. . . . The first
> duty of the legislator or the judge is to make clear, un-
> ambiguous statements, which not only experts, but the
> common man of the times will interpret in one way and
> in one way only. (1950, 114, 117)

What is at stake, however, in the law knowing what it wants? How can law be an agency for knowledge, particularly its own self-knowledge, and thus be the exemplary model for all other linguistic contracts and for language in general? And how is it that information theory and cybernetics can be a legislator of the legislation of communication—becoming a law of law, as well as a law over so many other fields of study? For Wiener, cybernetics is the law over so many other fields that its domain applies throughout the areas of not only technical systems but also social justice. As Wiener wrote in the 1950 edition of *The **Human** Use of Human Beings,* "The problems of law are communicative and cybernetic—that is, they are the problems of the orderly and repeatable control of certain critical situations" (117).

In both the 1950 and the 1954 editions of his book, Wiener repeatedly wrestles with the need to clarify the nature of this universal "law" of communication and information and to assert command and control over his own text that has this law as its theme. But Wiener's repeated attempts to define that law in ever wider circles result in ever more complex and chaotic notions of that "law" with every turn. Wiener's attempts to state the law of information theory and cybernetics—that is, the law of clear communication and the control that issues from that—ironically turns into an unresolved issue in his texts. Instead of being able to issue a clear and unambiguous statement of this law, the "law" metaphorically slips across different domains of discourse in order to more widely assert the power of this law. The metaphor of this law slips across technical and physical science to jurisprudence and economic problems of exchange value. In chapter 7 of the 1950 edition (chapter 6, 1954), "Law and Communication," in particular, it becomes difficult at times to tell from what discursive domain the term "law" is issuing from and to what domain it applies.

For Wiener, the essential problems of jurisprudence are interpretative, and it is the job of information theory and cybernetics to solve interpretative problems by clarifying economies of meaning. By conceiving of language in terms of information and communication and by conceiving of information and communication in terms of "systems" of constant exchange values that cross discursive realms or "currencies," Wiener attempts to keep the chaos of affects at bay in all realms of society and nature.[6] Wiener's reduction of language to a communicational and informational economy avoids an encounter with language or affects in terms of radical alterity, fracture, and chaos. His reduction brings language and being into a scale and economy of management and leads to Wiener's conjoining of the terms "communication" and "control."

As with information theory, cybernetics understood language and other affects in terms of systems engineering. As in Weaver's commentary on Shannon's work, the problem of meaning is scurried away by means of technical models and metaphors. Following information theory, the central problem of cybernetics is to reduce or eliminate the "no-man's land" of language as a whole,[7] that very historical "whole" out of which, as Heidegger put it, language speaks.[8] For what frightened Wiener (and he never ceases to remind his readers of this throughout the 1954 edition of *The Human Use of Human Beings*) is not simply noise or jam but the fear that meaning may not originate from some singular place or agency and may not be able to be re-presented in some other place or agent in the manner of a one-to-one correspondence and, since meaning may not have these qualities of presence and representation, that it may not be quantitative and therefore subject to the "law" of communication and/or control. If meaning and language as a whole were not, indeed, inherently subject to the assumptions and metaphors of communication and information theory, then Wiener's conception of a communicational state would cease being a democratic utopia and would begin appearing as a struggle between language and community and state power.

I would suggest, of course, that it is precisely this struggle that is at stake in Wiener's writings. His writings attempt to naturalize a technical model as a social utopia. That a communicational utopia is really a state of control is manifest in the very cyborg model that emerges out of cybernetics. The logic of cybernetics is that of systems engineering, which means that language and affects are viewed in terms of systems, quantitative values, message transmission and effects, and management and control. This logic makes cybernetics both a science (because it claims to be descriptive and predictive) and an industrial social practice insofar that it describes and prescribes societies as technical systems and it projects a logic of engineering upon both organic and inorganic organisms so as to envision a smooth space of cyborg message flows. The over-encoding of heterogeneous relationships establishes a predictive social structure modeled on the instrumental functions of machines and thus turns cybernetics into a form of "scientific" social planning complete with technological intermediaries.

For Wiener, cybernetics is not just "academic" or descriptive but has practical tasks aiming toward man's survival, namely, in terms of the fight against "nature's tendency to degrade the organized and to destroy the meaningful" (1954, 17). Cybernetic theory is immediately a pragmatic theory in the sense that its theoretical tasks fall under the directives of man's survival in hostile human and natural environments. The knowledge that is gained by the definition, classification, and prioritization of information of all kinds allows man to balance his needs against the challenges of society and the cosmos. As Wiener wrote: "To live effectively is to live with adequate information. Thus communication and control belong to the essence of man's inner life, even as they belong to his life in society" (1954, 18).

The science of cybernetics has, thus, two main goals: first, the discovery of the general law of communication in nature as a whole and its specific manifestations in different beings and events, and second, the survival of man. Furthermore, the accomplishment of the first goal serves the second. "Nature" is a series of messages or codes that humans must decipher, not only for the survival of humans but in order for humans to be most properly "man." Science, in other words, is a form of humanism in Wiener's work, and it is proper, therefore, that human society and beings, as expressions of man's humanity, also fall within the realm of scientific laws.

If cybernetics introduces the element of feedback and "learning" to positive science, it does so only insofar as it attempts (as in Otlet and Briet) to maintain the human as "man." Despite Wiener and cybernetics' cyborg vision, there remains a fierce, and even brutal, humanism of which information theory, cybernetics, and systems theory are but postwar symptoms. "Command and control" are socially prescriptive as well as scientifically descriptive terms in cybernetics, and the "science" of cybernetics cannot be separated from the politics of "man" in Western culture. The operationalized notion of beings suggested in the title *The **Human** Use of Human Beings* is, thus, a question of defining, abstracting, and generalizing the relationship among machines, man, and even other beings in terms of man's reason. In order to accomplish this (as was the practice in the Macy cybernetics conferences), other structural sciences are needed in order to "properly" define "man" on a global level:

> Père Dubarle is right—many more times than right—
> in his emphasis on the need for the anthropologist and

the philosopher. In other words, the mechanical control
of man cannot succeed unless we know man's built-in
purposes, and why we want to control him. (1950, 210)

As a general scientific law and practice, cybernetics provides an a priori
answer to the question of man's "built-in purpose": to control man through
communication in a hostile environment that, judging from Wiener's
political concerns, includes the hostility that issues from the "nonrational"
elements of humans themselves. The scientist, for Wiener, must look to
nature's laws for the "hows" of such knowledge. For Wiener, against the
arbitrary laws of Marxism and fascism, everyday man and the scientist
must have "faith" that nature has laws and must use that faith and its revealed laws to battle against irrational actions, language, and politics,
whether these come forth in the form of personal madness or the politics
of Marxism and fascism. Correspondingly, the scientist must work in an
environment that is free of political control and has as its chief principle
free communication so as to have maximum chance at discovering those
laws that correspond to rational communication and social justice, for the
discovery of these laws will ultimately secure man's own essential nature
and safety. Scientific faith for Wiener is, thus, a faith in the truth of man's
reason and nature's readability, that is, in the ability of scientific man to
correctly reproduce and represent—or, simply put, transmit and receive—
nature without "noise." Science, in other words, *is transmission,* and scientific progress lies in faith in the conduit metaphor (***Human*** *Use of Human Beings,* 1950, chapter 12; 1954, chapter 11).

Despite the detours of a postwar information theory based upon statistical certainty, with Weaver's and Wiener's works we arrive back at Otlet's
humanistically inscribed technological determinism. And with this we
arrive back at the paradox that a communicational state requires greater
amounts of standardization and control in order to produce greater
amounts of "freedom," so that the line between, for example, a "democratic" State governed by control looks little different from a totalitarian
State governed by discipline, save for the addition of more and more subtle
technologically and technically enabled devices of communication and
information and save for greater public acceptance of the virtues of communicational and informational space.[9] This latter acceptance was the goal
of Wiener's popular writings, which must be understood as agencies in the
development of a type of national and global politics and governance that
is defined by communicational and informational reason.

Is there another way than that of humanism and its subjectivity by, and through, political control that we may think the problem of affects in creating being and community? Is there a different ontology and episte-mology through which we may think becoming in-formed, through which we may think being and knowledge as becoming? In the next part of this chapter, I would like to push the problem of Wiener's communicational State a bit further and also introduce an ontology of information that leads to a different sense of community and politics.

Animal Songs

> Translation is so far removed from being the sterile equation of two dead languages that of all literary forms it is the one charged with the special mission of watching over the maturing process of the original language and the birth pangs of its own.
> —Walter Benjamin, "The Task of the Translator"

In "The Task of the Translator," Walter Benjamin engages the problem of communication and community from the im-possible zone of the babble of languages—precisely that area that communication and information theory identified as "noise" and chaos. The problem that haunts informa-tion theory and cybernetics is precisely the issue of repetition or transla-tion that information theory attempts to foreclose in the casting out of radical alterity—that is, that alterity that lies beyond the system's coding for recognition. For Benjamin in "The Task of the Translator," however, the tower of babble that we term "language" is the "call" to which we respond by speaking and writing and through other signs (70). Transla-tion, as a repetition of the message, for example, establishes the message in another tongue and gives a meaning to the original message that the origin or source may not have known it had. This retroactive attribution of meaning based on reply rather than intention, however, is more than the result of a "mistranslation." For Benjamin, meaning is rooted in and through series of responses that have no end and no origin. Any positive reading of identity, meaning, or affect calls for acts of auto-identity, auto-meaning, or auto-affection, which then demand yet more self-reflexive acts in order to recognize the validity of self-productions, ad infinitum. Inten-tion, as identity, in other words, is impossible to verify except by the pres-ence of an other, which in turn deconstructs intention or identity as a reflexive act by the subject alone.

Information theory's and cybernetics' conception of communication rests on the probability of choice within a system of language. Such a notion presumes that language is stable and that it is, indeed, predictable.

Such a stability to language is what Benjamin means in the above quote by the phrase "dead languages." Inasmuch as community might be understood as growing out of linguistic and other affective relations between beings, theories and beliefs about the nature of language and affects are important for understanding community. Communication and information theory, premised upon a one-to-one correspondence between one mind and another or one language and another, defines and prescribes a communicational sense of community based on identity, standardization, and systemic closure.

As has been seen with European documentation, Wiener's work, and as will be shown in Pierre Lévy's works, the social history of the rhetoric of information is largely comprised of utopian visions for information that envision a positivist communicational community on a global scale. Echoing such visions, politics no longer simply attempts to build an illusion of community out of an informational spectacle (as Guy Debord suggested) but now attempts the actual building of community through the rhetoric of the spectacle and through certain technologies identified as "information and communication technologies." In the name of the "global community," language is understood in terms of the communication of what is already known or is possible to know as information. Not only the products but the production of information and communication as the chief value for language and affect constitute the hegemony of the information society. Appropriating but then deepening Guy Debord's critique of the model of language offered by proponents of communicational ethics and communicational models of community (for example, Apel, Habermas), the Italian philosopher Giorgio Agamben writes:

> Whereas under the old regime the estrangement of the communicative essence of humans took the form of a presupposition that served as a common foundation, in the society of the spectacle it is this very communicativity, this generic essence itself (i.e., language) that is separated in an autonomous sphere. What hampers communication is communicability itself; humans are separated by what unites them. Journalists and mediacrats are the new priests of this alienation from human linguistic nature. . . . Even more than economic necessity and technological development, what drives the nations of the earth toward a single common destiny is the alienation from linguistic being, the uprooting of all peoples from their vital dwelling in language. (*Coming Community* 82)

The issue that Agamben addresses here is not so much machines per se as it is the social characteristics, history, and design of technology, not so much a future dependent upon certain information or communication technologies as it is a future embedded into technologies and into the social meaning, genealogy, and design of technologies by certain technical or instrumental understandings of technology, beings, language, and community. As Wiener writes in the beginning of chapter 5 of the 1954 edition of *The Human Use of Human Beings,* "phantasy has always been at the service of philosophy," mathematics being "the most colossal metaphor imaginable, and [it] must be judged, aesthetically as well as intellectually, in terms of the success of this metaphor" (95).

Wiener's purpose in this quote is to open up a discussion on the criteria for judging information theory's and cybernetics' worth in society. The criteria for this judgment, according to Wiener, is the ability of information theory and cybernetics to help man succeed. Success, as seen in Wiener's work, is a measure of the ability of the human to most properly represent itself as "man" in the face of chaos (that is, in the face of informational death). The task of information theory and cybernetics is, therefore, that of the clear transmission of man to man in the sending of reason into practice, thought into the world.

Despite the ontological and political manifestations of the conduit metaphor in information theory and cybernetics, it is the very nature of metaphor—that of a sameness founded upon the very fact of the non-identicalness of its repetition—that is the danger that information theory poses itself against. And in terms of its own metaphoricity, information theory appeals to its status as science and to a faith that the conduit metaphor is a metaphor that is not a metaphor and that the conduit metaphor can still the rhetorical slidings of language, can locate intention and understanding, and can bring justice to a world of difference. The conduit metaphor, inasmuch as it lies at the center of information, communication, and cybernetic theory, is, thus, the chief "scientific" metaphor of the tropic movement of language, and its job is to clarify and, indeed, circumscribe (or even banish from science) the formal or "literary" functions of language and restore to language its communicative functions.

By means of privileging the conduit metaphor as the essential model for information, Wiener attempts to preserve the intending subject against the dissolution of identity by "noise." For, if noise would become the standard for language and communication, how then would it be possible to distinguish truth from sophism, science from rhetoric, and the intentions of one person from the confusions of language in general? The utmost fear that Wiener harbors is that there may not be someone who speaks language, whether that one is speaking in the name of the classical subject, in the name of the law, or in answer to the question of "What is language?" Wiener's fear is precisely that of chaos—namely, that the individual may not be identical to itself, that community may not be identical to itself, and above all that language may not be identical to itself (and thus would be unable to authorize any forms of identity—personal, social, or even natural). In the name of preventing the meltdown of classical subjectivity and the State *as a state,* Wiener is willing to reduce time, space, and whatever sense of alterity necessary to that which is conquerable by information and its transmission. For Wiener, being is defined within an operational State-system. Beings, for Wiener, must be represented within a statistical system; otherwise they fall outside of the system's capacity to recognize them and thus are viewed as nameless, nonstatistical beings, constituting dangerous, unorganized affects.

Agamben has contrasted this communicational community with a notion of community made up of singularities of language and affects that unite, stabilize, and then dissolve among themselves, time and again, in radically heterogeneous becomings—singularities that he names by the specific but nongeneral term "whatever" *(qualunque):*

> The State can recognize any claim for identity—even that of a State within the State. What the State cannot tolerate in any way, however, is that the singularities form a community without affirming an identity, that humans co-belong without any representable condition of belonging (even in the form of a simple presupposition). The State, as Alain Badiou has shown, is not founded on a social bond, of which it would be the expression, but rather on the dissolution, the unbinding it prohibits. For the State, therefore, what is important is never the singularity as such, but only its inclusion in some identity, whatever identity (but the possibility of the whatever itself being taken up without an identity is a threat the State cannot come to terms with). Whatever singularity, which wants to appropriate belonging itself, its own being-in-language, and thus rejects all identity and every condition of belonging, is the principal enemy of the State. (*Coming Community* 86–87)

The problem Agamben points to is that of the State's desire to control beings through representation, that is, through the definition of beings and communities within known orders. For Agamben, beings are both (but never simply) products and agencies of language and affects, and they are only such beings inasmuch as they already exist through communities. Time and space emerge with beings insomuch as "being" always already means "being-with" (*"Mitsein,"* as Heidegger wrote in *Being and Time*). Community is not something that is attributed to beings but rather is something co-present in being; being and community are always co-intimate, co-immanent, and co-becoming. And it is this inherent community *responsibility* that is the greatest fear of the State, for it usurps the State's claim to grant community and being through its ultimate monopoly on defense, violence, and citizenship.[10]

Such a sense of communal responsibility is, therefore, not understood by the State as a genuine type of responsibility—one that the State claims to grant, regulate, and value within the institutional and semiotic forms of the State-system. And, inasmuch as affects are not yet formalized, that is, inasmuch as knowledge is still "in-formation" of becoming knowledge, the threat of "noise" is that it may be indistinguishable from "true" information.

The State-system has no difficulties with "opposition" if such is defined within its own operational terms—statistical norms appropriate and discard such opposition and bring within those terms those that serve the State best by being inscribed as "marginal" or "minority," granting them status as "voices" and "points of view." Critiques that threaten the logic or boundaries of the State's formal hegemony, however, are, as Agamben suggests, the real threat for the State-system. When the difference between "noise" and "the message" becomes uncertain, then the operational logic of the entire communicative system is threatened.

Therefore, as seen in Weaver's essay, the concept of "information" in information theory has a rather ambivalent structure, connoting both affects and organized representations. When information threatens to be "just" information, then the entire institutional and discursive apparatuses of the State are called in to stabilize meaning for the sake of "reason," "knowledge," and "common sense." Ultimately, that stabilization results in the exteriorization of informational affects that are not conducive with the language and being of the State-system.

The philosophical and linguistic problem of the "noise" of what lies outside of the essential state of man is thus directly related to the political stability of the liberal conception of the State. For, just as the being of the State is made actual only by the negation of marginal noise, so in the eighteenth century and through modernity the "question of man" has been answered via the negative category of "the animal" (even though it is admitted that man *is* an animal). As in Wiener's work, "nature" is that danger that demands that man find and have his identity in opposition to, and ultimately in domination over, the threat of nature's tendency toward chaos and entropic "death." The chattering of the apes, the lion's roar, even the hardness of the earth are all, thus, problems for man because they are possible threats to man's very being unless they become understood within the categories of man's knowledge and truth.

But humans *do* respond to nature's "noise." As threat or as wonder, as fear or as curiosity, affect forms a line of communication, resting against yet still escaping knowledge. Informationally, man becomes along with the animals. As an animal, man talks to the animals, and the animals talk to man—not according to the metaphysics of the conduit model and communication, not in terms of representation and understanding, but in terms of glances, touch, sounds, and replies. The category of noise is the trace of an affective joining and also of series of bifurcations that humans make together with other humans and with other animals. Specificity is marked by difference in relation to shared lines of affect, and such differences give rise to pragmatic senses of time and space.

If the noise of the universe cannot clearly be distinguished from the ability of the human to understand and, indeed, to express itself in nature (as in "society"), then how are we to limit the human to "man"? Or, once again, to approach this problem from within the logic of information theory itself, if the other's noise is so difficult to filter out from the message's signal—and, indeed, forms the "other" that gives the message its identity as the message, as intention, as representation—then how can we deny that this noise is not only inherent to but also prior to *any* sense of community? We then must ask if this relation between two or more bifurcating, continuously emerging and dissolving singularities—man and animal—is not the trace of the human *as animal, within the community of the animal.*

Jean-Luc Nancy has eloquently written on this problem of trying to limit the notion of community to "man":

> Community means, consequently, that there is no singular being without another singular being, and that there is, therefore, what might be called, in a rather inappropriate idiom, an originary or ontological "sociality" that in its principle extends far beyond the simple theme of man as a social being (the *zoon politikon* is secondary

> to this community). For, on the one hand, it is not ob-
> vious that the community of singularities is limited to
> "man" and excludes, for example, the "animal" (even in
> the case of "man" it is not a fortiori certain that this com-
> munity concerns only "man" and not also the "inhuman"
> or the "superman," or, for example, if I may say so with
> and without a certain *Witz,* "woman": after all, the dif-
> ference between the sexes is itself a singularity in the dif-
> ference of singularities). On the other hand, if social be-
> ing is always posited as a predicate of man, community
> would signify on the contrary the basis for thinking only
> something like "man." But this thinking would at the
> same time remain dependent upon a principal determi-
> nation of community, namely, that there is no commun-
> ion of singularities in a totality superior to them and
> immanent to their common being. (28)

If, as Wiener believed, the mathematical model of communication was a metaphor for the attainment of knowledge in civil society, in the man-ner that Plato's narrative of the cave was a metaphor for the attainment of truth in his Republic (1954, chapter 5), then what, we may ask, hap-pens to the narrative of the communicational community once it is re-leased from the narratives of rational identity according to man—that is, once community refers to the "in-common" affective relations of becom-ing beings rather than on a decided-upon realm of language and commu-nication? In other words, what happens to communication, information, and community when a society is founded *according to in-common needs and desires* rather than upon a mystification of individual abilities and intentions, powers and wills?

One result is that Wiener's scientific and social republic, founded upon communicative production, falls apart as surely as Plato's division of la-bor falls apart with the feared presence of actors in the Republic who can "mimic" one another, act in one role and then another, and speak a plu-rality of languages. Another result is that time and space must be viewed as results of affective relations in their becomings, not as ethereal medi-ums within which beings define themselves. Communication doesn't take place *through* time and space but *as affective relations* create the conditions through which time and space become meaningful for further affects.

Understanding this historicity of language and affect through the in-common becoming of beings leads to the conclusion that a communicational or informational utopia is both a practical and a regulative impossibility, because there is no possible totality for language and affect, or to put it another way, there is no communicational state against which one could measure language and affect for criteria of truth, justice, or being. The communicational State cannot arrive because its arrival is only possible through the very infinite becomings upon which it is premised.

Platonic narratives, such as Wiener's communicative republic based on a technological metaphor, have metaphysical, mytho-poietic, and ideological value in the service of founding and maintaining certain states of being and community, but they have very poor empirical value in terms of accounting for being, language, and affects and the role of these events in creating history and politics.

The problem with understanding the conduit metaphor as a model for a political or social state is that it models an ideological prescription, not a reality for either being or community. Consequently, social policy and research projects that are predicated on its social goals and epistemological foundations should be more critically examined than they are at present. A thorough critique of the conduit metaphor, for example, both in terms of its own logical presuppositions and in terms of its political and social functions, would lead one to question the foundations and purposes of many social and "user-centered" studies in information and communication research.

In the next chapter, I examine the communicative "virtual" utopia of Pierre Lévy that continues and intensifies Wiener's dreams of a global community founded upon notions of representation, intention, clarity, and the "free" exchange of information, though at a time when digital information systems and global hegemony have developed from their Cold War military roots to having thoroughly penetrated and encoded all levels of social and personal life.

4 ▪ Pierre Lévy and the "Virtual"

> World exhibitions propagate the universe of commodities.
> Grandville's fantasies confer a commodity character on the
> universe. They modernize it.
> —Walter Benjamin, "Paris, the Capital
> of the Nineteenth Century"

I f "information" is a trope for "science" that was understood in documentation first in terms of a positivist harmony (as in Otlet's works)
and then as a network of standards (as in Briet's works), and if it was
then understood in cybernetics as the transmission of standards, by standards, within networks dedicated to rational command and control, how
is it then understood today? What is information in a rhetoric of who "we"
are, in "our time"?

Obviously, we have characterizations of "information" and the "information age" from the mass media, digital technology corporations, poli-
ticians and the military, and various other interested futurologists. From
these sources, we believe that information has quantitative value, is exchanged and flows, and is that which one finds on the "information high-
way." Today, we believe that information both constitutes and combines
our educational, economic, and knowledge sectors. Information, we are
told, is the essence of our "age" and "our world," and, indeed, it is that
which makes us . . . well . . . "us."

Once these assumptions are accepted (usually without question), then
often the problem of information is one of assuring a "democratic" information policy for "us"; in other words, the problem of information is reduced to that of assuring that we will truly be modern in the sense of
having, at least, the capability of being fully informed. The haste by which
we move from a qualitative critical approach to a quantitative policy
agenda (for example, government- and media-led discussions on "the digital divide") for almost the entire problematic of the social and personal
meaning of information is truly remarkable. Even within academic hu-

manities research (an area that, in the recent past, has generated useful critical discourses), we hear positivist exhortations regarding the "newness" of information (most recently in terms of "hypertext") and the radical break this newness produces in regard to the rest of modernity and even to the history of Western culture in general. "Cyberspace" has become the signifier for this cultural difference said to be produced by digital technologies, and it has become a trope for a new historical formation—the "virtual age."

In this context, I will examine some recent works by the popular French theorist of "cyberspace" and the "virtual," Pierre Lévy. Lévy's work is well known in France, and it has recently appeared in English translation (1997). In what follows, I examine Lévy's analysis of cyberspace in two representative works, both of which have been translated into English: *Qu'est-ce que le virtuel?* (translated as *Becoming Virtual: Reality in the Digital Age*) and *L'Intelligence Collective: Pour une anthropologie du cyberspace* (translated as *Collective Intelligence: Mankind's Emerging World in Cyberspace*). In Lévy's work, the term "cyberspace" connotes "knowledge space," and knowledge space emerges in Lévy's work as both an object of information and as a space for objects of information. This duality of emergence occurs because, for Lévy, knowledge assumes the complexity of a problematic, inasmuch as knowledge is understood as "virtual." As we will see, the term "virtual" has a technical meaning for Lévy, borrowed from the French philosopher Gilles Deleuze's *Difference and Repetition* and from Deleuze and Félix Guattari's use of the term in their book *Anti-Oedipus: Capitalism and Schizophrenia.*

As "virtual," information or knowledge in the cyberage is characterized by Lévy not so much as an object but as a "quasi-object." Lévy's concept of a quasi-object is borrowed from Michel Serres (foremost from his book *The Parasite*) and from Bruno Latour (particularly from *We Have Never Been Modern*) and it connotes not just "objective" values for information but also values of community building and identity formation as well as object construction. In *Becoming Virtual,* Lévy makes use of an interesting example of the quasi-object and the community-building and identity-forming powers of virtual objects in cyberspace. Lévy's example is that of a soccer game, where the ball plays the role of being a quasi-object that acts as an "object-bond" for organizing a team of players. In what follows, I will attempt to tease out of Lévy's inherited concepts and this fruitful example some of Lévy's presuppositions about cyberspace that are invested in his work. I will do this by tracing back the intellectual roots of his central concepts and by analyzing his example of the soccer game.

Though Lévy's work can be polemical to the point of seeming like a manifesto (in the manner of Briet) or a utopian tract (in the manner of Otlet), this hyperbolic style brings to light some of the issues that are sometimes lost in more subtle narratives proclaiming the global virtues of cyberspace and the information age. Like Otlet, what Lévy's work sometimes lacks in academic "carefulness" is made up for in boldness and passion. But besides this, what is of value in Lévy's work are both the wealth of intellectual resources that he brings to bear on issues of cyberspace and the ways he bends modernist discourses and historical narratives to fit a certain popular rhetoric of information. As such, his writing becomes symptomatic of an assumed historical context for the notion of cyberspace, even as it attempts to account for this term through discourses of modernity. Thus, Lévy's writings, as seen against Anglo-American writings about cyberspace, are relatively rare examples of discussions about information that explicitly attempt to contextualize their arguments in a cultural discourse that includes but is not limited to policy and identity issues. Though issues of policy and identity are extremely important for Lévy, they occur within an examination of the "virtual" as a social and historical concept.

Examined in a historical and textual context, Lévy's writings nicely demonstrate how historical sources are "bent" under the pressure of what might be called ideological "strong attractors." In Lévy's writings, the rhetorical components of popular, ideological discourses that celebrate "virtual organization" and post-Fordist global capitalism are reinvested into French philosophy and Western canonical history so as to produce a popular work that claims to anthropologically show a coming communicational utopia. Because of the tremendous over-encoding of cultural life and social space by cybertopia visions of the late 1980s and 1990s and the difficulty of some of Lévy's original sources, it is sometimes an arduous task to fully untangle the web of ironies produced by Lévy's celebration of digitally led global capitalism, especially when he takes his terms from earlier Marxist-influenced texts (such as Deleuze and Guattari's writings). I must ask, therefore, for the reader's patience in this chapter as I attempt to suggest the levels of ideological force, textual perversions, and historical revisions that are at work not only in Lévy's texts but in other "information age" texts.

By using Lévy's texts to help analyze the contemporary rhetoric of information in terms of "cyberspace" and the "virtual," his texts become one series of historical examples for demonstrating the force that ideological power exerts in naturalizing not only vocabulary but also objects and subjects toward constructing a historical future as well as a historical past. Ideological power narrates reality and history by utilizing tropes that appropriate vocabularies, objects, and subjects from older historical series and from everyday events into historical series that become "inescapable" or "inevitable" futures, arising from "certain" pasts and presents. Only by such placements and displacements does power then historically justify itself and historically justify the "reasonable" range and logic of certain actions in "the real" as the only "practical" or sensible actions available to both policy makers and individuals. And only by working with an epistemology and method that seem to justify such transitions in the name of reason and research, or seem to accept the "facts" that result from such transitions ("empirically," or in the name of "practicality" or historical necessity), does power once again succeed in erasing the differences between historical agency and event and ideological encoding.

This chapter, therefore, is not just a topic for a specialist's interest, nor is it involved with questions that are strictly related to Pierre Lévy's texts. What is at stake in Lévy's tropes and claims is what is often at stake in acting "practically" in the "information age." That Lévy's work allows us (often unintentionally) a critical distance to examine these tropes and claims in a theoretical manner, rather than in a manner of being forced to obey the "inevitability" of historical law in our jobs or in our quest for knowledge through established routes of information, is a luxury that few practical texts about the information age now afford us. Whether a critical reading of Lévy's descriptive texts is welcome by the mode of composition of his texts is somewhat doubtful. That his texts, however, by the fact of their polemic and hyperbolic modes (as in Otlet's works) open up to such a reading is both the power and, in a sense, the fascination of his works. To echo the quote that began this chapter, in Lévy's works the commoditization of the world today in terms of information and the virtual becomes manifest and rational.

The "Virtual"

Oddly enough, Lévy's rather capitalist utopia of information in the "virtual age" heavily draws from two writers who were deeply engaged in leftist social movements of the 1960s through the 1980s: the French philosopher Gilles Deleuze and the French radical psychoanalyst and philosopher Félix Guattari. From Deleuze and Guattari's two volumes of their work *Capitalism and Schizophrenia* (*Anti-Oedipus* and *A Thousand Plateaus*), Lévy's work analogizes "information" according to Deleuze and Guattari's notion of the fluxes and flows of desire as it moves through centers and forms centers for the investment, capture, and transference of need. And from Deleuze's work, particularly his 1968 book *Difference and Repetition,* Lévy appropriates the concept of the "virtual," which he reads in terms of a Hegelian gathering of individual and collective thought. These two concepts—that of the flow of desire/information and that of its political unification in global "thought"—form the background upon which Lévy connects financial networks, technical networks, social organizations, and information and communication exchanges as series of metaphors of one another, building up to an "anthropology" of the "virtual age."

The first appropriation is fairly straightforward and is opened up by Deleuze and Guattari's own language. In both volumes of *Capitalism and Schizophrenia,* but particularly in the first, *Anti-Oedipus,* desire is understood in terms of being an immanent power *(puissance)* that capitalism co-opts, gathers, and exploits for purposes of extracting surplus value. At its most fundamental level, *Anti-Oedipus* constitutes a critique of the state system, which means that it constitutes a critique of power *(pouvoir)* as the controlling force for corralling and disciplining desire within states (political, psychological, and so on) where surplus-value is extracted from desire for profit. Subsequently, Deleuze and Guattari's critique of psychoanalysis follows their critique of capitalism insofar as it attempts to free desire from inherited systems of social organization (for example, the Oedipal family) that exploit the power of desire in order to maintain the state of power (for example, the father). Their Marxist critique both of psychoanalysis and capitalism is an attempt to articulate the mechanisms of power at the level of individual inculcation as well as an attempt to criticize an earlier, more traditional Marxist preoccupation with economic and superstructural analyses over personal, cultural, and familial analyses.

Lévy's *Becoming Virtual,* in particular, appropriates Deleuze and Guattari's notion of desire to that of information, using the common attributes of "flow" and "force" in both desire and information to set up a metaphorical equivalence. For Lévy, communicational or informational intent through new technologies is equivalent to that positive productive force of desire in Deleuze and Guattari's analysis. Consequently, throughout his work, Lévy reasons that "new technologies" work in a revolutionary manner against older technologies, forcing apart Oedipal capitalization and giving way to newer, more entrepreneurial forms of personal productivity that are, in a sense, more natural to human economy ("Isn't it equally possible, as Deleuze and Guattari suggest, that borderless, 'cosmopolitan' capitalism, in the sense of free enterprise, deterritorialization, and the general and unbridled acceleration of circulation, has been since its origin the state's secret nightmare? Is economy as a discipline anything more than the flattened, analytic form of the eternity of capital?" [*Collective Intelligence* 149]). Whereas Deleuze and Guattari's understanding of desire is based on a critique of all forms of capitalism, including liberal notions of money and exchange value (which, as seen in Weaver's and Wiener's work, inhabit information theory through the notion of "freedom of information"), Lévy's understanding of information in terms of desire claims that the information age is, essentially, revolutionary not only in terms of capitalist productivity but also in that productivity is essentially characterized in postindustrialism by knowledge exchanges that are exemplified in "virtual corporations" (*Becoming Virtual* 26) and by "human communities in the act of self-communication and self-reflection, involved in the permanent negotiation of shared signification" (*Collective Intelligence* 199). As I will discuss later on, Lévy's use of Deleuze and Guattari's work sets up a complex series of metaphorical exchanges between a philosophy of immanence and an ideology of capital entrepreneurship so that the current "technological revolution" and its service to global capitalism is seen as the "still imperfect embryo, coarse and one-dimensional, of a general system for the evaluation and remuneration of individual acts by everyone else" (*Becoming Virtual* 88).

The largely Deleuzian origins and meaning for Lévy's use of the term "virtual" are more complicated to pursue, but the manner by which this term in Deleuze's *Difference and Repetition* becomes appropriated within a discussion of the virtual in terms of digital technology reveals the manner by which Lévy constructs a particular, largely Hegelian conception of community as well as history. Because it is the key term in Lévy's writings, it will be useful, therefore, to spend a little time exploring the complexities of Deleuze's meaning for this term and Lévy's appropriation and transformation of that meaning within popular connotations today.

As Brian Massumi writes, the notion of the virtual is a very central but often overlooked concept in Deleuze and Guattari's coauthored works, and there it follows the trajectory announced in Deleuze's earlier solo work, *Difference and Repetition* (34). In the fourth chapter of *Difference and Repetition,* "Ideas and the Synthesis of Difference," Deleuze develops the notion of the "virtual" as distinct from a notion of the "possible." For Deleuze, the difference between the virtual and the possible follows a difference in the process of iterative unfolding between what Deleuze terms the "Idea" and that of the representational concept (*Difference and Repetition* 191).[1] For the representational concept, the notion of "repetition" signifies the production of objects out of what is *possible* within the confines of the idea. Contrarily, the virtuality of the Idea "has nothing to do with possibility" (191). For Deleuze, "Ideas are complexes of coexistence" (186). Analogical to, for example, biological chromosomes, Ideas may be understood "not simply as places in space but as complexes of relations of proximity" that constitute potentialities (185). These complexes are affected by their relationship to other complexes and by their actualization as specific events. Thus, the repetition of the virtual Idea (its "actualization") is an unfolding of the immanent potentialities of the Idea in relation to the specificities of other unfoldings.

Though the unfoldings of the Idea occur in relation to an immanent set of potentialities, they are undecidable in the exact directionality or sense *(sens)* of their unfoldings because the actual specificity of their unfolding determines their expression. Ideas may unfold in manners that explore the multiplicities inherent in the Idea, or they may just reconstitute the Idea into a representational concept. For example, for Deleuze and Guattari in *Anti-Oedipus,* the Oedipus complex is a virtual Idea inasmuch as its sense must be constituted by repetition in actual social events. These events may proceed in the direction of demonstrating neurotic formations through particular libidinal investments in classical social Oedipal structures and events (the traditional family, social forms of sublimation, debt to the father, and so on), or, to the contrary, they may proceed in the direction of demonstrating schizophrenic (or other comparatively "psychotic") formations wherein all the social structures through which the Oedipus complex is built are dissipated and spread out in social space (129). In both cases, the immanent tensions within the Idea of the Oedipus complex (for example, familial relations, heterosexual and homosexual libidinal investments and identifications, a temporality of inheritance, and so on) unfold, though in two totally different ways—the one ("possibility") toward structuralizing those tensions through libidinal reinvestment in symbolically repetitious forms and manners (for example, compulsion neuroses where symptoms are symbolic embodiments of Oedipal conflicts) and the other ("potentiality") in dissipating those tensions across structures of social space so that their actualizing instances may become agencies for the reconfiguration of those tensions (for example, Schreber's psychotic projections of the concept of the father across notions of God, the sun, and the power of his anus).[2] While the neurotic unfolding of socially produced Oedipal tensions preserves a certain configuration of those tensions not only within neurotic symptoms but also within the very "cure" and institution of psychoanalysis, the schizophrenic (or more generally, the psychotic) response has the virtue of working through some of the tensions and contradictions of the Oedipal Idea—*as a complexity*—in ways that both change neurotic structures and, at the same time, exploit the complexities of the Oedipal Idea in manners that representational repetitions fail to do.[3] In Deleuze and Guattari's reading of schizophrenia, psychoanalysis is itself undone by the distribution of Oedipal characters by objects in social space in such a manner that prevents their reintegration into the Oedipal conception of, for example, the traditional family. Whereas "possibility" is a socially conservative form of repetition, "potentiality" is understood to be a relatively radical form of repetition within Deleuze's notion of philosophical expressionism. By means of his concept of "potentiality," Deleuze maintains a historical accountability and a durational unfolding of history while freeing historical events from determinisms rooted in representation (for example, Hegel's notion of history as dialectical progression). For Deleuze, the return to the complexity of the Idea in its actualization stands in stark contrast to an actualization that finds its "strong attractor" in ideology.

Now, for Deleuze and Guattari, objects (for Deleuze and Guattari, "objects" may be "semiotic" as well as "physical") may be "entranceways and exits" (*A Thousand Plateaus* 13) because they have a certain material autonomy. This materiality of objects is what gives Ideas their factuality, that is, the materiality of objects works toward the actualization of the potentiality embodied in Ideas. The notion of the future, for Deleuze and Guattari, is thus composed of both a form of historical duration and a form of radical temporality, the latter of which *gives* time to history. In Deleuze's *Difference and Repetition* and in the chapter "Tenth Series of the Ideal Game" in *The Logic of Sense,* this dual notion of time as Chronos and Aion, respectively, is symbolized by the roll of the dice, a peculiar game in which all the potential throws of the dice, past and future, are brought to bear in a single roll. The Idea of "dice" contains all the potential combinations of a roll, and it is the roll that makes actual those potential combinations.

For Deleuze, Ideas are problems in the sense of being complex questions, what we might call "problematics." Deleuze specifies that the unfolding of problems within the Idea involves actual questions that direct the problems within the Idea to particular forms of unfolding. Further, whereas the form of questions in the possible is characterized by the notion of a reply or answer made up of concrete solutions, the form of questions in what Deleuze calls the "virtual" or potential is characterized by solutions that are themselves questions or problems within the potentiality of the Idea's complexity. Citing the discussion of repetition *(Wiederholen)* in Heidegger's book *Kant and the Problem of Metaphysics* (which had earlier been raised by Heidegger in *Being and Time*), Deleuze points out that a series of possible solutions is only one substantiation of what is potential, that is, it is only one direction or sense of the complexes that make up an Idea (*Difference and Repetition* 201). For Deleuze, as for Heidegger, the most interesting questions are those that continue to exploit the possibilities of an Idea through a form of questioning that returns again and again to the complexity of an Idea (qua problematic). Thus, for Deleuze (and in this aspect, for Heidegger), there is an essential difference between the structure of questions that seek, and have, certain *possible* answers ("solutions") and questions that must return again and again to the *potentialities* within the complex of the Idea (for example, that of the question or problem of justice). The essential difference between these two types of problems marks the difference between the possible and the potential (or "virtual"). The term "virtual" in Deleuze's work involves an immanent unfolding of potentialities. It involves questions that are not exhaustible but that come to appear as problematics in their actualizations.[4]

Now with this explanation of the terms "virtual" and "actualization" in the writings of Deleuze and Guattari, let us return to Lévy's use of these terms and concepts. Lévy's use of Deleuze's (and Guattari's) notion of the "virtual" has three dominant aspects. First, Lévy's stress upon "virtualization" reverses Deleuze's emphasis upon the movement from the virtual to the actual (*Becoming Virtual* 26) with the consequence that the priority of the Idea's essential complexity and unfolding not only in time but as time is lost. For Lévy, instead, the problematic and undecidability of the virtual is preserved within the hermeneutics of interpretation. An important result of this change in the notion of the virtual is that Deleuze's expressionistic philosophy gives way to a Hegelian-like dialectic between questions and answers, concepts and their understanding. This logic of dialectic and, consequently, of hermeneutics (along with such issues in the hermeneutics of communication as identification and standardized language) is not only absent from Deleuze's work but is in fact exactly what is brought into critique by Deleuze's work. Though a dialectical actualization is important for Lévy, it is "virtualization" on a global scale—as the idealistic *Aufheben* of the individual and "concrete" into the globally collective and "virtual"—that is Lévy's main interest. Here, Lévy turns Deleuze's expressive idealism not only into Hegelianism but also on its head by rendering the ideal as the global *telos* of digitally mediated presence.

The second point where Lévy deviates from Deleuze's conception of the virtual (again, in a very Hegelian manner) is in his privileging of the virtual as a manifest historical and social space, insofar as the term "virtual" designates both a historical phase and a universal collective space. Despite Lévy's demands that the "virtual" is an event whose foremost quality is that of "deterritorialization" (a term that Deleuze and Guattari use for indicating desire's—as well as capitalism's—capacity to rupture traditional boundaries), Lévy's historicism and "anthropology" of the virtual, whereby the "virtual" becomes the most recent progressive moment of technological innovation, means that virtuality ceases to be an analytical concept and instead becomes a reified term for historical events within a canonical form of historiography that is characterized by the concept of progress. Moreover, beyond this historical and teleological reification, the spatial reification of the virtual in terms of its being a global network means that Deleuze's notion of the virtual has been, in fact, conceptually "territorialized," not only within a very traditional method of historiography but also within a reified geographical entity (namely, the earth understood in terms of "the global"). In sum, ironically, the virtual, because of Lévy's historical and spatial redefinition of Deleuze's term, has never left what Lévy himself characterizes as the second, previrtual space of human development, namely, that characterized by "territory" (*Collective Intelligence* 210).

This peculiarity that Deleuze's "virtual" has become in Lévy's writing the structural and canonical space and time of the "virtual" is demonstrated by the fact that the actualization of the virtual for Lévy means that the virtual "must still grasp onto some physical supports and become actualized here or elsewhere, now or later" (*Qu'est-ce que le virtuel?* 18).[5] For Deleuze, the "material actualization" of the virtual means that the virtual becomes real as an event in either an intellectual or a physical sense, and thoughts, as well as physical events, are "material." The important criterion for material actualization in Deleuze's work is not that there is a "physical support" but rather that there is a crystallization of affects and forces resulting in other particular affects and forces. When the dice are thrown, for example, certain numbers appear. What makes this an actualization of the virtual is not that this or that particular pair of dice are thrown but that there is the expression of the potentialities of dice in the event of the throw. Those potentialities cannot be said to lie exclusively in a particular pair of dice but in the plays of chance that are inherent within throws of dice in general.

The importance of Lévy's reduction of material necessity to physical necessity is that physicality connotes a type of concreteness in dialectical relation to a universal collectivity of thought in technically mediated "virtual" space ("Access to the intellectual process of the whole informs that of each part, individual or group, and nourishes in turn that of the whole. In so doing we make the transition from collective intelligence to intelligent community" [*Becoming Virtual* 145]). The Hegelianism that Lévy acknowledges in his work (*Collective Intelligence* 223), namely that of attempting to understand collective intelligence as the reconciliation of those classic Hegelian categories of thinking and being, singularity and universality, and knowledge and identity, also haunts his understanding of the relationship between the virtual and the actual. Despite Lévy's claim that the end result of these relations is the production of pluralization and heterogenesis (*Collective Intelligence* 223), the end result is not an open heterogeneity of becomings and beings but rather a utopian closure upon what beings can be. This closure is symbolized in Lévy by the soccer team and the game of soccer, a sense of "community" where rules and play, and identity and community, resolve their dialectical antitheses through a common object (the soccer ball), objectives, and standards.

In the next section of this chapter, I look more closely at Lévy's metaphor of the soccer game, paying attention to its formal construction and how that formal construction shapes the nature of the object. What is at stake is the manner by which technologies and other materials are encoded as the future and then act as tropic and material determinants of the future. Epistemologically and politically, the contrast that I wish to draw is between treating materials as informational and transformative objects (in the manner of being "entranceways and exits") and subjecting them to historically prescribed codes or "centers of calculation" that not only direct their genealogies in certain directions (for example, toward "communication") but also turn them into rhetorical devices for organizing other senses of social space. The process of this "virtualization" of informational objects from that of material agency to speculative agency is unwittingly analogized in Lévy's metaphor of the soccer game that comes to deny the formal conventions and the material grounds that lead the soccer game to be a game and the ball to be a soccer ball. If "virtualization" is, then, the tropic reification of material objects and social events by formal structures of power (that is, it is a product of ideology), it has strong similarities to Briet's argument that materials must be named within orders of knowledge. And if this is true, what is the difference between Lévy's futurology for technological objects and social space and Briet's insistence that documentation must fit itself within the ideology of "science"? What, in other words, is the difference between our virtual future and ideological narrative? Where is the materialist analysis to this virtualization of our future, and why is there so little discussion of the slippery rhetoric of the "information age"?

Rhetoric, Quasi-Objects, and Social Form

Lévy's textual arguments for a utopia of virtual collectivity take place against specific modernist narratives and events from which they attempt to distance themselves but which they repeat in their historiographical and rhetorical form. Just as Otlet's vision for the role of "the book" in bringing about world peace developed in reaction to antagonistic national alliances in the late nineteenth century and the clash of those alliances in World War I, so Lévy's explanation for the "virtual" political and financial economy of cyberspace takes place against the historical background of modernist fascism, mass media, and mass or crowd psychology. Throughout his work, and in particular in his discussion of the two types of groups involved in a soccer game, the crowd and the team (*Becoming Virtual* 151–53), Lévy is attempting to distance his reading of collective thought in the age of global electronic networks away from those classic modernist readings of community that theorize community in terms of social bonds built out of a logic of sacrificial exclusion (in the manner of René Girard's analyses in *Violence and the Sacred*) or out of a logic of identification and its mimetic relation to transcendental law (as in Freud's analysis, foremost in *Totem and Taboo*). Lévy attempts to distinguish a politics and an economy of the virtual from mass forms of organization, production (such as Fordism), and communication in order to promote a "new" vision of community founded upon the communicative and informational possibilities of virtual technologies.

In the section of *Becoming Virtual* that deals with the metaphor of soccer, Lévy writes:

> How can we make the transition from collective intelligence, which is an inherent feature of humanity, to intelligent communities, which deliberately optimize their intellectual resources here and now? How can we create a society that is flexible, intense, and inventive without founding the community on hatred of the foreigner, a sense of knee-jerk victimization, or a relation to transcendent revelation or some providential leader? Is there a way for personal acts and resources to operate in concert without subjecting them to an alienating exteriority? (151–52)

In Freud's influential descriptions of modern society based on analyses of crowd psychology, for example, Freud both criticizes crowd formations and, paradoxically, founds psychoanalytical theory upon hypnotic suggestion and affective contagion. As Mikkel Borch-Jacobsen has argued, Freud's notion of *Gefühlsbindung* (the social bond built from mutual affective relations) approaches a political model of fascism insofar as it proposes that community arises from the process of identification between a *Masse* of individuals and their leader. In Freud's analysis, the totem or group object is the symbolic token of the leader who is revered as a transcendental figure. This symbol, for Freud, is, of course, the ambivalent figure of the father, a figure both revered and hated by the group. In Freud's *Totem and Taboo,* it is precisely the killing of the father that binds the "primal band" of brothers into a society through the introduction of mass guilt, but it is also this killing that raises the father to the level of being a transcendental force in the development of law and conscience.

Though Lévy does not, of course, use the parental or even a human figure as a token in the construction of the mass nor the objects of information and communication technologies as objects for subjective identification, he does use information and communication technologies as metaphors for community and as organizing central tokens for the formation of social groups. (Lévy characterizes the role of information and communication technologies here in terms of its creating an "object-bond.") Lévy's technologicalization of the primal figure transforms the historical form for modern society: instead of connoting steadfastness, it connotes speed and change; instead of connoting a nationalist mass, it connotes a potentially international mass; and instead of appealing to national myths for social guidance, it appeals to other "networks" (financial and organizational) as well as to the technological tools themselves as metaphors for community. For Levy, each of these elements—speed, mass, and navigational tools—contributes to the creation of a new "knowledge space," to a new "collective brain."

As we saw in Otlet's work, documentary collectivity, standardization, and communicational exchange constitute the "world brain" that Otlet and H. G. Wells saw as the salvation of mankind. For Briet, dynamism, internationalism, apparatus, and connectivity constitute the "new era" of "scientific" modernity. For cybernetics and the information dreams of the World War II regime, "science" or man's rationality is metaphorically figured by the individual computer or computer bank. Similarly, the new age of Lévy's "virtual" is constituted by these old dreams, their historiographic form, and their narrative tropes (for example, "No less than the utilitarian search for information, it is the vertiginous sensation of plunging into the communal brain that explains the current enthusiasm for the internet" [*Becoming Virtual* 145]). Though Lévy sees himself as announcing the end of the modern, the modern has never left "information." The "information age" occurs again and again, its repetition masked by the cultural truth and banality of its particular rhetorical pronouncements.

Forgotten in Lévy's narrative dreams for the virtual are Guattari's fears that "any metaphorical representation of the drive, whether topical, dynamic or energetic, risks arbitrarily deforming the aporetic character of the crystallization of these existential Territories, which are at once incorporeal, intensive and multicomponential" ("Schizoanalytic Metamodelisation" 67–68). The tropes and technologies privileged within a given "information age" overwrite all other social forms for existence. For Lévy, all technology is based on substitution, on "twisting and doubling reality" (*Becoming Virtual* 116). Becoming thus ceases to take place in the manner of those existential and material aporias of actualization that Guattari mentions, and, instead, existence becomes mediated through technologies of representation and tropic representation of those technologies that, as Guattari and Eric Alliez suggested in their essay "Capitalist Systems, Structures, and Processes," will act as the rhetorical means for capitalist semiotic recoding. In Lévy's digital critique of modernity, the rhetorical functions and operations of information and communication technologies in structuring material objects and persons into the political mass are forgotten, which means that tropes of information and of "the global" are repeated again and again.

Information and communication technologies are not just representational or "virtual" at the level of presenting visual or auditory simulacra; they themselves may constitute instances of representation or virtuality insofar as they are substitutional or tropic figurations that mediate the future both technologically and semiotically. As such, the terms "internet," "cyberspace," "information," and the "virtual" often substitute for one another in popular discourses and in Lévy's texts because these terms do not denote particular objects of information technology but rather are representations of certain privileged social mediations and of visions of social communication and social order in the present and in the future.

In popular rhetoric, technical machines may, for example, act as figures for reading back onto human personal and social spaces those qualities that are attributed to machines in the first place: speed, connectivity, and navigational mastery. The logical qualities of networked machines are read back upon the social subject not because machines accurately represent the form of those subjects but because they act as tokens for mediating personal and social identity into established forms. Far from allowing heterogeneous singularities to occur and to establish independent or "free" autonomous zones, the trope of the network, for example, advocates social and personal identities based on individuals with standardized or "shared landscapes of meaning" (*Becoming Virtual* 142). Such human landscapes (to mention just one ecology) then allow technical networks to act as communicational devices for creating further "networked" organizations. Technological devices thus become social forces for constructing human societies based on the tropic qualities attributed to such devices. Technological devices are more than simply mechanical agents for enforcing social power; they are important rhetorical and semiotic devices and as such are fundamental (as Briet recognized) for the primary stages of colonization, especially within modernity's information- or communication-based economy.

Thus, technical connectivity acts as a trope for personal and social organization in order to allow communication to occur rather than "static" or "misunderstanding." Technical networks are not in themselves socially communicative, but as social tropes they have the power to construct—not only technically but also socially—a future based on a vision of social connectivity and communication. Further, their objective appearance as technology lends them a privileged status in regard to the future within an ideology of rational and technological progress (that is, in terms of an ideology of "science").

Without this investment of social power in the informational or communicational object, without this prescription of an "inevitable" future following certain tropes of information and information devices, such devices or technological networks of such devices lose much of their social power; they become merely one type of machine among others, one device among many, one apparatus in the production of knowledge among many, one form of knowledge production among many. Each device then becomes specific instead of general: "cyberspace" must be enumerated and analyzed according to specific types of devices rather than as a *social* whole.

As a projection of a social whole, as a rhetorical token for communicational consensus (and as Habermas has shown, as this constitutes a return to Enlightenment reason), the informational network device is not simply a technological device but is both a harbinger of the future and a trace of prior social determinations of power. Those very qualities that Lévy and such theorists as Bruno Latour find so endearing in what is called the "quasi-object," namely, that it both mediates and traces social networks, is less a quality of the empirical object itself than of prior movements and codings of power, resulting in centers of calculation that cast their shadows across varieties of social landscapes. As we have seen in the case of Latour's example of the exotic bird specimen, the bird specimen both constitutes and traces the network of Western exploration and Baconian science. But it does so only so far as the individual specimen constitutes a trace of a form of reason that not only holds but also insists that the world can and will be represented, and indeed preserved, by the collection and comparison of specimens outside their local domain.

For Lévy, technological networks, organizational networks, and, more generally, social networks link easily with one another and share one another's objects because they share standardized formal qualities among them. But quasi-objects are not "quasi" simply because they, as objects, function across ontological types or series (institutions, organic bodies, machines, and so on). Rather, they are "quasi" because they are representations of social desires that utilize objects in order to bring about goals of social organization. The success of one scientific model over another, for example, is not simply a matter of contemporaneous contestations; its technological and empirical objects are symptomatic of a series of projections toward what will count, what will organize, and what will be the objects that both organize and model the future. Often, the social traces that an object makes in its circulation are not simply of its past or even of its present but of its future. Social forms advance metaphorically and metonymically through history, and such forms speak through the meaning we attribute to objects and the uses we foresee for them in the future.

Thus, the symbolic projection of the object goes three ways: into the social meaning and the technical construction of the object itself, into the construction of the future, and into the structuralization of singular events and beings into recognizable articulations and "individuals." Psychoanalysis gives the name "part-objects" to those parts of bodies that are intensely constituted by libidinal investments (for example, the breast, the penis, and so on). As is well known, this term's genesis can be traced from Freud to Melanie Klein to Terry Winnicott's "transitional object" to the Lacanian *objet petit a* and to Deleuze and Guattari's critique of the notion of the "part-object" in the previous writers' works. As was mentioned, for Deleuze and Guattari, the object constitutes "political options for problems . . . entranceways and exits" (*A Thousand Plateaus* 13). In those writers previous to Deleuze and Guattari, objects (as part-objects) were generally understood in terms of representation, lack, and supplementation. Part-objects represented the fulfillment of lack in the subject's psychic organization. Only for Lacan does the part-object go further than the representational order itself, transversing the Lacanian symbolic and imaginary fields and then standing as remainder in a "real" that cannot be recuperated. As remainder, the *objet petit a* both drives and is a limit to desire.[6] And as remainder, the part-object becomes separated from the symbolic body and begins its genesis as a libidinally invested object per se in a social field.

Deleuze and Guattari continue the Lacanian displacement of the object beyond the symbolic field, but then they go further than Lacan by claiming that the object has a libidinal role other than that of being a symbol for lack. As an assemblage of forces, the object constitutes a means of repositioning the subject in the subject's becomings. The book or computer, for example, is not simply an "exteriorized brain" (in the manner of Otlet), nor is the internet simply a "collective brain." Rather, each object has, as Guattari makes clear, a technical as well as a social lineage, and it constitutes an actualization of particular and ever-changing potentialities by its affective engagements with other subject/objects (Guattari, "On Machines"; "Machinic Heterogenesis"). As a complex event rather than as a representation, the object constitutes a complex site for actualization. Together with other agents of affects—such as human agents—the object becomes a machine of production, constituting what Deleuze and Guattari term "a line of flight" for subjectivity. As such, the object does not mediate a relationship between the subject and the world; rather, it shares a certain form of mutually mediated becoming with the subject. Rather than being a substitute for a subjective lack, a representation of an absence, objects are points of engagement for a subject's co-becoming with "objects." As such, objects do not simply stand outside the symbolic; instead, they institute affects that are both signifying and nonsignifying (*Anti-Oedipus* 47).

In continuing to their materialist analysis of objects, the effect of the structuralization of objects through networks of power was a problem that deeply concerned Deleuze and Guattari. For example, the investment of normative Oedipal forms into the economy of family relationships (that is, "mommy, daddy, and me") often gives rise to neurotic formations that are shared by the individual and by the social collective.

Guattari, following his and Alliez's concern with the social outcomes of capitalism's process of semiotic encoding, was particularly concerned with the effects of the educational structuralization of objects and then their projection and introjection into the developing child or adolescent. The reduction of "learning" to certain types of institutions (schools, churches, the family, "community" organizations) and the prioritizing of certain object-tools for affective engagement and production (words rather than music, chairs rather than moving objects, writing instruments rather than speech) may be recognized as the prioritizing of certain contexts, modes, and products of learning within the being of the child for the purposes of serving capitalizations of desire and labor in the future. Even more important than these contexts, modes, and products are their semiotic inculcation in the general life of the child by means of habits, class inscriptions, moral rules, and the ability to recognize certain forms of sense as information or knowledge and others as not (what Foucault characterized in terms of the construction of a "society of control"). In this context, the traditional concept of "information" is that of formalized encodings that are recognized as "informational" by their being embedded so deeply in institutions and practices of knowledge that those contexts or frames disappear, leaving the appearance of an auto-affectively produced, self-evident object of knowledge. "Continuous education," for example, in an information culture works upon the prior interiorization or "introjection" of established structures for learning and for recognizing informational value-content beyond the context of the original institutions. It is not based on expanding knowledge or in contesting the public space of knowledge but on learning or training according to already established and authorized modes and codes—in other words, it is learning qua "information."

For Guattari, the object can be constituted as a part-object within the institutional structuralization of the body. The problem that Guattari raises is not simply that of the projection of meaning upon objects but also how the meaning of the object is formed, what is done with that, and toward what ends. These are questions that involve first of all a critical understanding of objects as representations of social space as well as within processes of psychological introjection. As in the case of education, Guattari argues that "what matters is whether one uses this semiotic apprenticeship to bring together power and the semiotic subjugation of the individual, or if one does something else" ("Desire Is Power" 22). What Guattari means by the term "semiotics" here is that of a series of affects that are both signifying and nonsignifying. What Guattari raises is the problem of how to utilize objects in ways other than introjection, and he questions the production not only of "clear" articulations and other affects but also of standardized social and personal subjects. The question of physical structures for semiotic encoding is taken to the level of language as a semiotic whole. The "deterritorialization" of the traditional classroom by information technology, for example, does not hold, by any means, the promise of a different type of classroom, because the problems of education can be masked even more subtly in digital formations and standards. The revolutionary promises of information and communication technologies must be measured against formal controls upon language that lie at the heart of early modernist mass formations, not against technological innovation.

For Freud, the defining moment of personal formation is that of primary repression. In psychoanalysis, primary repression occurs at the moment of the articulation of the father's threat of castration due to the son's desire for the mother. For Freud, all other repressions and sublimations of desire are secondary and are repetitions of the force of this threat in a retroactive manner that Freud termed *"Nachträglichkeit."*[7] As Lacan points out, the effects of primary repression are to erect the symbolic order within the subject's own psyche, therefore formalizing the future play of signs within an already defined but totally forgotten field of action. The value for objects is thus forestructured by a process of force and repetition that defines the value of objects within a political field whose interests are more often than not highly conservative, if not reactionary.

Guattari's critique of institutional introjection follows a critique of primary repression inasmuch as it raises the issue of the meaning of the informational and communicational object as a formal question within a social play of power. For Guattari, representational identity bespeaks a prior sketching out of the social field and also bespeaks, in the recognizable—in the "clear and distinct" (to use Descartes's characterization of truth)—enunciations of the subject, the effects of introjection and personal/social structuralization.

For Guattari, "individual" enunciations differ from "singular" enunciations inasmuch as the former refers to enunciations emanating from a self that is socially structured according to bourgeois notions of individual (molar) personhood within capitalism, while the latter is indicative of a more molecular congruence of forces and affects. As we have examined in the previous chapter, a common understanding of the communicative function of language is that which follows the conduit metaphor, a model that proposes connectivity not only by means of grammatical and syntactical standards but also by means of a standardization of identity at the productive and receptive "poles" of the communicative message. Guattari's critique does not involve a total rejection of structuralization; rather, it involves a questioning of its use. In the domain of language, for example, Guattari raises the issue of the cultural dominance of the so-called communicative function of language over the so-called poetic function,[8] inasmuch as the former is based on the conduit metaphor:

The preeminence of a mechanistically determined information flow tends to result in a generalized dissolution of previous existential territories. . . . In these conditions, the poetic function is more than ever called upon to recompose artificially rarefied and resingularized universes of subjectivity. It is not a matter of its transmitting messages, empowering images as a ground for identification or formal patterns as a prop for design procedures, but of catalyzing existential agencies capable of gaining consistency and persistence at the heart of the actual, mass-mediating chaosmos. ("Texts for the Russians" 3)

Despite the importance that Lévy claims for deterritorialization via the virtual, Lévy's understanding of deterritorialization is limited to exchanges of standardized identities within a formally defined field. Thus, this limitation strongly controls the nature of subjectivity and the political radicality of such. Such terms as "deterritorialization," "heterogenesis," and "becoming" in Lévy's texts have meanings different from those of the same terms in Deleuze and Guattari's works, where they refer to events involving becomings through radical alterity. For Lévy, in contrast, it is radical alterity that threatens the informational and communicational object as an object that has utopian promise, and thus, alterity must be seen as a border or limit to information and communication. As in Wiener's work, in the name of preserving meaning and social order in the present, and in the name of arriving at a communicative utopia in the future, not only must the object itself be kept consistent and readable but also its meaning must be repeated through countless tropes. The informational and communicational object thus traces not only a promise of an inevitable future but also what must not be thought in that future. To put this in the language of Walter Benjamin, the "aura" of the informational object masks the dark side of its production and of its productive social force. The information and communication object, elevated to being a cultural and rhetorical trope, is a transcendental sign of the existence of a social field of communication where its value is produced and assured.

Like Wiener, for Lévy the limits of (communicational) law must be kept in view; otherwise, communicative connectivity will wither away with the loss of personal and collective standards for productive and receptive agency. In this manner, the organization of the body (personal and collective) is analogous to the state of language, inasmuch as the "poetic function" (or radical deterritorialization) in the social and psychological realms must be understood as a sign of a "boundary" that promises only "alienation" and "amputation." For Lévy, this identification of an alterity beyond identity—as a warning sign—is an ethical and civic responsibility. Alterity, as a threat to identity, must be marked as a border in order to preserve ethical purpose and civic law:

> The boundary between heterogenesis and alienation, actualization and commodity reification, virtualization and amputation, is never clearly defined. This boundary must constantly be estimated and evaluated by the individual, to help determine how to conduct his life, and by society, to determine how to structure its laws. (*Becoming Virtual* 44)

For Lévy, the meaning of the object depends on "a contract, a set of regulations, an agreement" (162–63). The appearance of the object is "inseparable from a specific form of social dynamic" (163). These regulations and agreements—in sum, these forms of social dynamics—give the object its "dynamism" and make the collective space itself "dynamic, emerging, cooperative" (143). The social effect of cyberspace is thus to promote "connections, coordination, and synergy among individual intelligences" (144), and this is even more productively done "when individuals or groups are able to identify one another in a virtual landscape of interests and skills" (144).

For Lévy, one such social dynamic occurs through computer-mediated communication (or "groupware") software (such as Lévy's "Knowledge Trees" software) that has a "figure-ground" topography, "where information is always presented in context" (143). In the twentieth-century tradition of communication and information theory, standardization is the key to constructing information, that is, for defining contexts through which information seemingly autoaffectively appears as content. The "figure-ground"/"content-form" relationship is part of the aesthetic design of data into information according to the norms of representation.

The key to understanding the play of the (quasi-)object or the object-bond and its seeming empiricism in Lévy's work and those of his sources lie here as well. For Serres in his book *The Parasite,* the game of "hunt-the-slipper or button, who's got the button *[furet]*" (225) (whereby a player is "it" based on the stoppage of a collective passing of an object from one person to another) is analogous to the social construction of the psychological self through the (collective) language game that the pronominal "I" circulates within. Similarly, for Latour, scientific facts are like frozen fish:

"The cold chain that keeps them fresh must not be interrupted, however briefly" (*We Have Never Been Modern* 118). Likewise, in Lévy, the notion of "shared landscapes of meaning" is both a necessary condition and an effect of the quasi-object. The landscapes for meaning in a soccer game, for example, are the rules of the game, the goals of the game, the financial forces acting upon the teams, and even the physical grounds upon which the game is played. These landscapes constitute the "background" upon which the game is played, and apropos the object-bond of the soccer ball, they are what give the ball its meaning as a soccer ball.

But through such examples that Serres, Latour, and Lévy give, we may ask, what is empirical about the (quasi-)object in these cases? What is lost (or gained) if the collective passing of the button or the *furet* does not follow the rules of the game? What happens to Latour's fish if the measuring index of the thermometer is lost (for example, we mistakenly measure thirty-two degrees as freezing with a centigrade thermometer)? Why is Lévy so afraid of that "uncertain boundary" that is, indeed, a "disembodiment" of communicative meaning and standardized identity (*Becoming Virtual* 144)—a disembodiment that, according to Deleuze and Guattari, is the exact and necessary ontological condition of a molecular becoming, of a becoming (and thus, to some degree, a confusion of identity) of the priority of the play *before* the game, of the roll of dice rather than the role of the soccer ball?

Indeed, we can only say that such empirical facts, like that of quasi-objects, remain such only when held within indexes that grant them a certain status and being. A certain objectivity is granted them according to certain assemblages of language games and other indexical systems that form centers of calculation and centers of naming. Empirical objects such as quasi-objects appear in the social sciences, for example, only because such "sciences" are built from canons of language, measure, and techniques. (We may add, here, simply as a hypothesis, that the case may be quite different in the physical sciences where proof often includes the testing of material resistance to change). As Briet argues in regard to the origin of documentary fact, documentary facts are such facts because they are referential signs to materials that are indexically located in social systems, and insofar as such systems are deemed to be "scientific" discourses, the included referential signs there come to be deemed "scientific" facts. "Facts" are indexical signs within productive systems just as the named elements of soccer are. The role of documentary and social science fact is not to pose material resistance against representation (as, for different purposes, occurs in both the physical science and the critical arts) but to enter material into the play of representational language games and instrumental techniques.

Thus, the "quasi-object" in its constituted/constituting duality is nothing other than that which is defined within a set of institutions and signs to play a central role in establishing such-and-such institutions and signs a domain over materials. The quasi-object is no more an empirical fact than any other social fact—than the "facts" that Briet so brilliantly saw as being tokens within indexes, pointing from the past toward the future. The quasi-object is a semiotic marker crossing liberally heterogeneous institutions and ontological types that are conjoined and held in place by their sharing of a code or a series of codes for locating and defining an object and its functions. And the "smoother" the space for the circulation of those tokens—that is, the more totalizing the logical, aesthetic, and social constructs—the more those tokens may appear to not only trace but also identify those spaces. Money, for example, very naturally seems equivalent to finance for Lévy, because money is understood as part of international finance. But take Lévy's metaphorical equivalent for finance, that is, language, where utterances can indeed be *not* understood—especially across cultural distances and historical gaps—and then, like Briet, the necessity of standardizing a linguistic "currency" becomes urgent for communication and the circulation of linguistic messages to occur.

Language objects and social spaces often are not continuous with one another; rough translations across series of languages and social spaces occur as "language." Software design standards intercede across various social spaces and languages so as to construct contexts of figure and ground in order for representational information to occur. Software design is, thus, the formal aesthetic construction of a representational collective or community of users, using a combination of technical and social standards. Both software objects and users become tokens or players within a set of institutional assumptions that make up the representational space of software. It is not a coincidence, therefore, that much user-level software occurs in the form of games. Software tokens symbolize—in an exemplary fashion—the projections and the temporal assumptions of games. In Lévy's work, virtual social spaces and their objects and subjects resemble game tokens because the representational nature of games forestructure virtual space.

Ultimately, quasi-objects trace nothing other than the projections of their representational meaning, whether those projections have epistemological, institutional, or personal origins. Quasi-objects can be displaced insofar as they are material objects and offer resistances to representation, but this in turn challenges and even changes the role and the meaning of the quasi-object in a linguistic or social procedure or "game." A soccer ball can be a bird's nest, but this object is then no longer a central token in the game of soccer. An "I" can be a pronominal token in a poetic rotation of pronouns in a text,[9] but its ability to be a token for self within a "language game" of personal reference in ordinary language is then challenged or displaced. Quasi-objects have no empirical standing outside institutional representations and prescriptions and the futures that such structures impose or demand.

It is not by chance that Serres and Lévy elicit the game of soccer to exemplify the token nature of the quasi-object, nor that Serres in *The Parasite* chooses a Wittgensteinian example (the indexical properties of the first person pronoun,[10] which Wittgenstein himself developed by thinking of "language games" on the model of the game of chess) in order to exemplify a "quasi-subject." And it is not by chance, as it were, that Deleuze chooses a wholly different "game"—one that is lacking rules and has the most minimal of physical objects (that of the game of dice)—to propose a different type of ontological model. Far from being a simple example, in Lévy's writings, the trope of the rule-governed game reflects the formal boundaries of language, understanding, and society in Lévy's notions of virtual organizations and community. Lévy's soccer ball is not so much an example of informational and communicational objects, but, rather, in a funny twist, informational objects are examples of soccer balls. And soccer balls, in turn (when, like information and communication devices, used "correctly"), are parts of events that are governed by institutionally established social practices. The use of such objects according to certain manners and means (informational and communicational objects in order to communicate and inform; soccer balls to play soccer with and not to use as birdhouses) both symbolizes and prescribes certain modes of normative social practices, now and in the future.

Thus, in Lévy's writings, quasi-objects in general, and informational and communicational objects in particular, are not simply descriptive of landscapes of meaning but are historically constitutive, historically symbolic, and historically prescriptive of those social, cultural, and historical "landscapes" inasmuch as the rules and relations of those landscapes were in power before particular quasi-objects even appeared. And since such objects are created vis-à-vis semiotic and rhetorical means of encoding based on substitution, it is difficult to understand what purpose it serves to be so cautious about those "uncertain boundaries" *(limite indécise)* (*Qu'est-ce que le virtuel?* 31) that are, of course, symbols of an endless play of substitution, other than the fact that Lévy finds it necessary to enforce those boundaries as specific and definite limits to the play of substitution in general in order for information and the virtual world to exist as definite events and objects.

If, in the final analysis, quasi-objects are not tokens of empirical exchanges nor truly harbingers of a future but instead are tropes for power relations that determine normative social and linguistic "games" and the habits, borders, and rules of the games now and, even more important, in (and as) the future, then we must now ask exactly what those important determining institutions, standards, and discourses are that allow the "virtual" game of communication and community to be performed, especially *as history.* What are the institutions and the institutional tropes that determine the game of communication in the "virtual" future? How do "we" all become "team players" down to our very "I"'s in "our history" of the "information age"?

The Games People Play: Inscribing Self and Group Through Finance and Soccer

If quasi-objects are given their identity as objects within structures of play that are projections of power, then what types of institutions or institutional discourses are privileged in Lévy's rhetorical construction of the "virtual"? In *Becoming Virtual,* two illustrative examples stand out as both symbols and institutional vehicles of communicational reification: that of post-Fordist or "virtual organization" team management and that of sports teams. Each of these examples of teams practices a form of communicative control and exchange that constitute language and event in terms of regulated exchanges, standardized subjective identities, and identifiable objects.

The dominant character of each of these teams is the problem of "management," because, as we have seen, quasi-subjects, like quasi-objects, are not simply empirical structures. Established institutions, rules, and habits control the appearance, identity, and language of teams, their players, and their objects through constructing the conditions for, and the substance of, knowledge and communication. Such control occurs through defining knowledge according to certain standards for affective relationships, exchanges, and vocabulary.

As I have argued, quasi-objects within organizational or epistemic structures are most fruitfully understood as historical projections of power. Subjects (or as Serres more accurately calls them, "quasi-subjects"), understood as group and personal identities within post-Fordist production, are conceived in terms of teams and team players, and their self-representations are forced into such directions so as to "correctly" fit within this ideological order. That Lévy's understanding of virtual community is in terms of teams, and that such a vision would seem so natural to us today, sadly says a great deal about the hegemonic forces behind the ideological introjection of the team metaphor throughout those structures of the family, the educational "cohort" (a term whose military origins date from the ancient Romans), and even the organically conceived "self" of everyday psychology. Such linguistic control provides the bridge through which corporate control proliferates and is maintained throughout formerly private spheres, thus subjecting all areas of social life to what Guattari and Alliez identify as capitalism's semiotic encodings.[11]

For Lévy, "finance . . . is one of the most characteristic activities associated with the growth of virtualization" (*Becoming Virtual* 68). Money is an exemplary instance and symbol of virtual communication because it represents a common object in the play of global exchange (68). Furthermore, Lévy accepts the information age truism that knowledge and information not only are the leading *goods* within the current economy (70) but also are "virtual" goods in that they, like money, are based on public exchange, nondestructibility in their consumption, and "nonexclusive appropriation" (88). By means of a naive understanding of money as a quasi-object in global exchange,[12] and by means of claiming that language is exchanged through communication, Lévy analogizes language along lines of a certain vision of global finance. "Inevitably," therefore, virtual communication is both supportive of and supported by capitalist global finance. Neo-liberalism's "freedom of information" becomes equivalent to capitalism's "freedom of exchange" across a global sphere.

Consequently, for Lévy, finance is important in the construction of the "social mind" because it brings individuals into play on a global scale through the quasi-object of money/information in the global economy. Individuals are brought into play according to knowledge and information, which, in the new "information economy," have the quality of financial goods. One of the foremost purposes of computer-mediated communication software is to act as "free markets for a new economy of knowledge, which provide members of a community with a synthesized view of the range of skills possessed by the group and enable them to locate their identity as an image in the knowledge space" (*Becoming Virtual* 143). Networked spaces provide opportunity for an economy to emerge that is no longer based on institutions of certification and hiring but on "a form of self-promotion, involving qualitatively differentiated abilities, by independent producers or small teams" (*Collective Intelligence* 4).

For Lévy, these small, self-promoting cohorts or individuals follow the design of "collective intelligence." They are intelligences "whose subject is multiple, heterogeneous, distributed, cooperative-competitive, and constantly engaged in a self-organizing or autopoietic process" (*Becoming Virtual* 128). Such intelligences follow a "Darwinian" model in their self-organization. For Lévy, Darwinian systems have the capacity for "self-directed learning" through their ability to select from the environment "novel items" (129). Selection, combination, and variability are elements of both "human groups" and "individual species." For Lévy, the market is an autopoietic "Darwinian machine" whose intelligence is greater when businesses and consumers are also such machines (129). Darwinian actors in the autopoietic mind of the virtual follow a logic of "association, exchange, and rivalry" in utilizing intellectual "weapons" for "competing within a globalized economic space" (*Collective Intelligence* 5). Lévy's collective or virtual world brain, thus, is a result not only of dialogical relations among participants but of a global "free market" of players. The "collective brain," then, is not just any collectivity but a product of intellectual free-market "excellence," as it were.

Of course, the "free market" is neither "free," nor is it made up of just "winners." Darwinian capitalism produces "losers" who are little comforted that they, indeed, did play in life's World Cup or that they stand the honor of being in, as Lévy proudly puts it in the truly amazing conclusion to his book, "humanity's new home" of the virtual (*Becoming Virtual* 187).

Indeed, money is also not simply a "virtual" object in the free and smooth flow of exchange, as the liberal theory of money would have it, for money is a product of actual labor (intellectual or otherwise)—a "product" that represents and enacts vast inequities of wealth and exchange. It not only symbolizes those inequalities but also enacts them. Far from circulating in a smooth space of seamless exchange and currency translation, money is the product of striated, violent, and contradictory material forces of production and consumption—for, if it were not, it would have no value within capitalism. Analogously, but for different ontological and historical reasons, communication or language as a whole is not virtual or "smooth" either, whether on the internet or in everyday interactions. Language practices constitute rough, striated series of spaces and disjunctures that rupture and change language in both diachronic and synchronic ways so that language both continuously grows and necessitates everyday translation. Language creates understandings from misunderstandings and misunderstandings from understandings. It is *always* and can be nothing other than *material,* whether or not it occurs through so-called virtual (or more accurately, digital) technologies. Its exchanges are always rough, interpretative, and temporal.

But along with the money game and the language game, the soccer game must also be said to be material; its "virtual" smooth space of "play" is only a dream, based on a series of impressions of power and a series of specifically managed physical resistances (the resistances of materials in terms of their hardness, speed, and slowness). The game of soccer is most essentially based on the need to keep the ball in play according to rules. Players are chosen, others are dropped or benched, the ball is inflated to a certain level, and the grass is clipped to a certain height. What falls to the wayside of these planned affects is tossed outside the soccer "grounds." We can neither say that the soccer ball is simply a trace of the players nor that the players, in their strategies, are players of any other sport than soccer. A notion of "soccer" is applied to the ball and the players, thus making them objects (and subjects) of "soccer." Autopoietic developments not only depend on a set of rules but also take place upon, and within, the "grounds" of the soccer game, conceptually and physically separating the players from the crowd. The free-play of the players and the game are within tightly defined rules and standardized roles for identities and enunciation, and the spectacle is conducted for profit and for community identification.

One of the effects of this division is to create two different sets of groups. Both groups, however, form themselves around a symbolic object. For the crowd, they gather as the team's crowd—for or against the "Panthers" (the teams are so often named after totemic animals!). For the players, they gather around the ball, as much as the ball and their success at playing the ball will gain them (as in American collegiate football) the game ball—a ball that will symbolize that the Panthers "crushed," "killed," or "slaughtered" the "Lions." The game ball, here, doesn't constitute a neutral object but is the symbol for mastering the intricacies, the strategies, and, of course, the rules (both formal and informal, on the field and in the clubhouse and in front of the media) of the structured game. Though it is true that the collective bond of the team is not built through sacrificing the ball and eating it (*Becoming Virtual* 154), both the crowd and the players bond through mastering the game, a game that may have been cooperative in terms of team group formations but was zero-sum competitive in its process and goals. In the end, the sport is mastered by being mastered by the game, and the game ball is claimed only so that the sport and the ball will reappear in the next season and act as the inherited transcendental demand that spurs the Freudian "brothers" to bond once again so as to attempt to master it. The team celebrates the Darwinian fact of their game by claiming the game through the symbolic object of the game ball (and, of course, in the prize money), and the fans devour or mutilate the totemic flag or mascot of the opposing team.

Any autopoiesis in the community of the sport-game here is purposeful, determinated, and affectively constructed by forces outside the play itself. Loosen the formal constraints on the appearance of the play of the game proper (during the off-season, for example), and a larger Darwinian space appears in which the game's other motivations become apparent (players compete with each other for money and prestige, media networks fight over future television rights, owners hire and fire managers and players to generate more revenue). We may say that the sacrificed totemic "animal" or father assumes a variety of forms here in order to cohere, through sacrifice, those other "teams" and economic classes below it. If the quasi-object traces anything in the soccer game, it traces the subject's debt to a desire larger than the subject's, a game that is anything but autopoietic, and like all sport today, to a produced, consumed, and sustained myth of being and becoming that shapes the behavior and values of future generations.

Lévy's "teams" of finance and communicative speakers do no less than produce a myth of life. What he envisions is not a utopia but a dystopia. He describes not a natural future but a product of neo-liberalism's society of control that encodes us from our very first words, that tropes us from birth to death.

Information: For Fun and Profit

The world of the stadium as the world of normative language games as the world of the "virtual" show themselves as frames for the constitution of informational and communicational objects and subjects. Such frames are products of forces of power affecting the value and "proper" relations of the tokens involved. Though Lévy presumes to define virtual beings in terms of potentialities, he ends up defining potentialities as Deleuzian possibilities because he dreams of a communicative space wherein language and identities are based on standardization and standardized exchange. The notion of "standards" frames the concept of the "object," as well as the subject, within a predesigned space that Lévy sees as "community."

If the worlds of post-Fordist capitalism and sport are not simply random examples of contemporary power in, and constitutive of, society but instead are two formal and thematic exemplars of it, is it any wonder that social spaces that wish to picture themselves as being on the "cutting edge" frame themselves in these terms on both organizational and linguistic levels (not only in the actual worlds of business and sport but in education, politics, internationalism, and militarism; in short, in any "practical" or "professional" field) and that Lévy, too, so eagerly appropriates these realms as tropic figures for the "virtual" and for his future utopia?

In our everyday lives, we are told that "the world" needs "solid team players," "information," "new ideas," people able to "push the ball forward," people who can communicate "precisely" and "clearly." Perhaps. But "the world" is based on "miscommunicational" communication, a language that evolves poetically, soccer balls that are mistaken for birdhouses, language and identity that are affective but in no way presume to be "communicative" or stable. And if we ask which is primary, there can be no debate; the world is not rational. I am not suggesting here any romantic counternarrative to the tropes of the "virtual." No counternarratives are necessary to prove a primacy beyond the global community or the virtual. Games, digital or otherwise, are social constructs and constitute tracings, territorializations, and surveillances over a range of materials and events by acts of power. They are born out of displacements of other activities and meaning that are reterritorialized into structures, normalized into certain senses of social and personal being, and then narrated and mythologized as "natural" and exemplary.

The virtual, in Lévy, is born of rhetorically and socially generated displacements and projections onto technological objects and human subjects in order to form a futuristic order that then can demand of the social its fuller alignment into that order—as the inevitable future led by technological advancements. These displacements are processes of substitution that bring a social "vision" into view within the dominion of the representational—an aesthetic/cognitive structure held together and naturalized by power. In this sense, Briet's insight was deeply profound: the technological future resides within the cultural event of "science." Within a rationally coherent and socially supported ideology, the future is manufactured and sold as "fact," and us along with it.

The "virtual," "the global," "the information age," "the dynamic," "the new," the value of "communication" . . . Lévy's texts utilize these terms as rhetorical devices to advance a future. But these terms are rhetorical substitutions for present powers beyond Lévy's texts that attempt to advance themselves. How these terms "capture" objects and most of all subjects is the critical question so often avoided in information studies throughout the cultural and academic domains, as information studies are driven by "policy studies" that are critical only after the acceptance of these terms, after the acceptance of a future driven by these tropes. The problems of the social production of these terms and of the exact nature of their material referents is rarely asked. Who is the "we" for whom this is a "new age"? Whose history is this? Whose "future"? Whose "world" or "global" is this? How are these "whose" produced—both individually and collectively—as the future and as historical agents in the so-called information age? The information age—or at least this one—may be upon us, but it has never really been seriously critiqued publicly. Its language had been produced long before, so that "we" could become an "us" in the "information age." Must we wait for the next information age, or—as in the past—will we have already forgotten this one by then?

In the next chapter, I will look at critical interventions to the information age that began before World War II. These interventions pose forgotten questions about the cultural and material production of information and communication, and (especially since they were posed by well-known theorists) they also pose the question of why they have been forgotten, especially within a discourse on the information age. Once again I ask, why is it that certain information becomes transmitted by each information age—namely, that which allows their historical repetition? And why is it that the information age is so good at forgetting that which was contrary to its "vision" before?

5 ▪ Heidegger and Benjamin: The Metaphysics and Fetish of Information

As seen in the preceding chapters, professional and authoritative discourses on information during the twentieth century have tended to project upon society and history—past and future—social forms that mimic technical forms of information production. The "information future" in professional and authoritative texts is thus a rather cheerful, optimistic, or at least determinate future. Inasmuch as such texts also repeat early, similar pronouncements and their tropes, they come to speak in a rather singular voice about the nature of information in the future, forming a rather curious tradition of information history made up of tropic repetitions. As witnessed from European documentation through Cold War information theory and cybernetics and into the age of the "virtual," information determinism forms a discursive web that unites agencies, institutions, and cultural agencies across society toward the promotion of an information future. The hegemony of these professional and cultural authorities determines not only what will be understood as the content of information but also the forms of knowledge that are to be privileged as "information," the policies that will govern knowledge, and the meaning of the "information age."

In what follows, I return to the late 1930s, the period that was the height of documentation and that witnessed the blossoming of mass communication in the West, in order to look at some criticisms that engaged information determinism. During this period, when information technologies were being used to develop mass national movements and the technologies of war, some largely forgotten discourses were critical of what has become known as "information." These discourses argued for thought and social movements founded upon other principles than those of representational unity and systemic transmission.

Insomuch as these critiques were focused on the formal characteristics of information, they pointed to mimetic relations between technical production and social production. And insomuch as both Martin Heidegger's and Walter Benjamin's critiques were those of information as representation, they attacked, in their different ways, the social machinery whereby "information" was produced and reified. Further, each of these critics found that the very nature of history and historical being lay within the problem of information. For Heidegger, information was the latest phase in the operationalization of being, including its very historicity. For Benjamin, public information was part of the commodification of history according to the bourgeois image of industrial progress. Each critic attempted to demystify the developing concept of information and the reification of knowledge that was occurring in mass culture and through technical organization.

Otlet's major texts were written during the middle 1930s, a period that witnessed the political fruits of a tremendous growth in certain types of information and communication technologies. Otlet's visions of multimedia information technology (such as the portable information screen mentioned in chapter 2) and of world unity through such technologies and their representational aesthetics were partly an outgrowth of earlier developments in telephony, microfiche, radio, and television and partly an outgrowth of late-nineteenth-century and early-twentieth-century advances in systematically organizing and arranging information (for example, decimal classification codes, international standards, and international organizations and libraries). But Otlet's visions did not just emerge out of these technological and technical advances. Along with other world documentation proponents such as H. G. Wells, Otlet expressed these visions out of anxiety over the threat of another world war that, ironically, was made possible by those communication and information technologies that they promoted.

Of course, 1937 was part of a decade that witnessed the utilization of global technologies and philosophies for reasons other than world peace. Technical reproduction, including that of information and communication technologies, helped create the conditions for and then drive both persecutions and war in this period by broadcasting discourses and technical transmissions over mass social spaces and by linking communications into communicational systems. As the confluence of technical reproduction and mass mobilization became ever more apparent in the coming war that would engulf both Europe and its colonies, the technological determinism that fueled Otlet's optimism about the future threatened the very nature of "the future" itself for millions of people. The information age of the 1930s became increasingly difficult to distinguish from the machinery of totalitarianism, global politics, territorial expansionism, and war mobilization. The technological, social, and historical forms of modernization that gave Otlet faith in the progressive nature of documentation and information at the same time threatened to engulf Western culture and society in flames.

The crisis of the cultural meaning of technical reproduction was, of course, felt in other intellectual circles than those professional circles involved with technical development. Since such technical reproduction involves not only technological processes but also processes of human technique and social organization, questions regarding the meaning of technical reproduction in culture involve such seemingly diverse phenomena as popular culture, journalism, social management, and urban planning—in brief, the whole range of those cultural and industrial agencies that generate and are products of modernism. Thus, it is not surprising to see such issues raised as philosophical issues, as well as more general issues in critical cultural theory, and to see the outcomes of such analyses as other than further positive exhortations about the future social utopia of a technology-based society.

Heidegger's and Benjamin's works are well known in philosophy and social theory. It is striking, however, that in the midst of this celebrity, Heidegger's critiques of information and cybernetics are little highlighted and that Benjamin's materialist critiques of technical reproduction have not been very well tied to earlier dadaist and Soviet avant-garde critiques of bourgeois historical production. Whereas Heidegger's work approaches information historiography through the method of a counterhistoriography rooted in a critique of metaphysics' construction of being since the ancient Greeks, Benjamin's work seeks to disrupt information's historical progress through a critique of the narrated mass image itself, attempting to "blast" it out of its smooth systemic production and to return it to its material contradictions and possibilities. However different these critiques are in terms of their methodological roots and their disciplinary and political orientations, they are part of a body of works that exhibit symptoms of a significant historical trauma. For these writers and others (such as Robert Musil and even Freud in a social reading of his concepts of trauma and repression), the period from the beginning of the twentieth century up to World War II was a period of cultural trauma or shock that needed accounting for in terms of philosophical, social, literary, and psychological writings and actions. It is significant, I believe, that Heidegger and Benjamin relate this shock to the emergence of a systemic, representational, and public form of knowledge now better known as "information" and to the processes of modern "communication." This theme of shock, at least as a historical and cultural phenomenon, was largely forgotten after World War II, at the very moment, as seen in Wiener's work, when information and communication were naturalized as the accepted form of knowledge and language throughout both public and private life.

The sections that follow in this chapter, therefore, attempt to provide an introduction to Heidegger's and Benjamin's critical engagements with modern information and its production. My attempt here is to critically reengage the traditional historiography of information both from the aspects of historically abandoned critiques and of critiques that have a major focus on informational history, historiography, and historicity. By means of this recovery, I hope to suggest that there have been critiques of information and communication in history outside the positive tradition discussed in the earlier chapters and that these critiques have been abandoned both in favor of and through further positivist accounts of information and communication.

By situating my analysis on texts that originate in 1930s Europe, I also suggest that there are political ramifications for the type of historical tradition of information outlined earlier—namely, that a naive historical understanding of information in modernity is part and parcel of a naive understanding of history and that together these mask attempts at hegemony and domination, from the level of mass force to the inculcation and control of everyday life. Both Heidegger's and Benjamin's works trace these events of modernization at national and cultural levels, and they suggest that the direction of such modernization is toward domination at the global level. Thus, their works are relevant to us today, both as historical examples and as still valid critiques.

Martin Heidegger and "The Age of the World Picture"

Martin Heidegger's critique of the effects of modern information and communication technologies could be said to begin in earnest with his public lecture "The Age of the World Picture" ("Die Zeit des Weltbildes") (1938), though the central concepts within this lecture were evident a decade earlier in *Being and Time* (1927). With this lecture, Heidegger's critique of the method of modern science is joined with a critique of machine technology in the context of a metaphysical account of technicality as a whole *(techne)*. The themes that occur in this lecture continued after World War II through such seminal works of Heidegger's as "The

Question Concerning Technology" ("Die Frage nach der Technik" [1953]) and "The End of Philosophy and the Task of Thinking" (1964).

Heidegger's critique of modern science and its philosophical precedents centers on a concern with the positivist manner through which beings and things are presented as true within forms of representation and within a systematic linkage of those forms in modern culture. Insofar as the re-presentation and re-production of beings occur by techniques and technologies whose contexts of production are not well accounted for in terms of those beings' "factual" appearance, such beings are said by Heidegger to be brought forth in terms of presence or as information. Thus, Heidegger's critique of information involves a critique of both production and method in their establishment of truth according to an aesthetics of representation. In contrast to this production of knowledge as representation, Heidegger argues for a sense of knowledge and truth whereby beings remain uncertain for scientific method. Heidegger not only attempts to preserve the value of interpretation for method and understanding but also to preserve time and space as constructed values within being and truth.

In contrast to Otlet's and Briet's technologically determinate vision of a "scientific" future, Heidegger argues that such a vision poses a fundamental danger to humans and to other beings. For Heidegger, this danger lies in the vision's underlying belief that man can represent all beings and their relations. Thus, Heidegger's critique of positive science engaged it in terms of the metaphysical tradition of representation and how that tradition comes into fruition through aesthetic devices for representation and their social domination through systems of communication.

Since this theme begins to emerge in the relatively nontechnical language of Heidegger's public lecture "The Age of the World Picture," this lecture makes a convenient jumping-off point for considering Heidegger's critique within a larger social context. However, while my focus upon this lecture has the advantage of sketching Heidegger's concerns about technical reproduction, modernist science, and information in relatively easy-to-understand language, it has the disadvantage of not completely indicating the depth of Heidegger's critique within the context of his most essential thoughts on ontology, truth, language, and art. On the other hand, though, that Heidegger's concerns about the social effects of technology in his 1938 lecture (and these concerns remain remarkably consistent throughout his career) can be narrated largely outside Heidegger's technically "philosophical" concerns and language (and are, in fact, narrated as such in "The Age of the World Picture") suggests a certain social engagement in Heidegger's work that cannot be restricted to philosophical rhetoric proper. Be that as it may, the reader should be forewarned that in the following analysis I can indicate only the philosophical depth and complexity of argument that unfolds from "The Age of the World Picture" throughout Heidegger's later writings.[1]

In "The Age of the World Picture," Heidegger argues that modern science and machine technology are the most important characteristics of the modern age and, indeed, that they constitute the metaphysics of the modern age. For Heidegger, the modern sciences are foremost characterized by the mathematical and physical sciences. Such sciences provide the model for what it means to be "scientific" in modernity, expressing theory, method, objects, and subjectivity in terms of representation. For Heidegger, there are two aspects of this form of science that dominate other forms of modern research and knowledge: quantitative measurement and the systematic relating of objects in logical systems of representation. Machine technology both is a product of these two aspects of science and reproduces this form in its own production (that is, the machine is made up of singular and recognizable parts assembled in distinct relations to one another, and machines are characterized by their ability to reproduce distinct objects whose relations to one another are easily predetermined). With the triumph of the mathematical physical sciences, observation and description become quantitative activities, and beings become understood as objects that are present to humans in a clear and distinct manner. True knowledge is understood in terms of the object's clear and distinct presence in the mind of the thinking subject. As a clear and distinct re-presentation, the object becomes countable and factual knowledge.

For Heidegger in "The Age of the World Picture," the dominance of this type of criteria for knowledge shapes the understanding of beings across all domains of knowledge. For Heidegger, the essence of modern research consists in a projection (*reissen:* tearing, sketching out, or design) of beings out of a phenomenological totality and a making present of those beings as empirical entities within a structure or system of knowledge (that is, as particular species of bird or plant, particular behaviors, particular types of men, and so on). (This process of indexical naming is precisely what Suzanne Briet saw as "scientific" about documentation in her *Qu'est-ce que la documentation?*) Thus, as Heidegger argues throughout his work, through metaphysics human beings become "man," the subject who observes nature as an object *(Gegenstand)* that is opposed to *(Gegen-)* and distinct from man, utilizable according to its ability to fit man's rational categories and tools.

According to Heidegger, rigor and disciplinary methods in the sciences emerge from and reinforce certain foundational object-ive projections of nature *(Grundrisse)*. The *Grundrisse* gives rise to certain research divisions within science and forms the basis for a modern scholarship composed of researchers ("men of a different stamp" from older types of scholars, according to Heidegger) who act according to institutional research agendas, produce findings, and display an industriousness rooted in the busyness of meetings and conferences (for example, producing and receiving information at meetings, publishing and reviewing such information according to the needs of publishers and scholarly institutions, and the like). "The scholar disappears," Heidegger writes. "He is succeeded by the research man who is engaged in research projects" (125), much as the artisan was followed by "scientific" modes of management and production.[2]

Researchers, as the thinkers of the modern age, work upon carefully sketched out, defined, and represented objects and their phenomena according to the methods, tools, and techniques deemed appropriate by the field's founding *Grundrisse*. "What is taking place in this extending and consolidation of the institutional character of the sciences?" Heidegger asks. "Nothing less than the making secure of the precedence of methodology over whatever is (nature and history), which at any given time becomes objective in research" (125). This "making secure" of research, in turn, guarantees that research remains always industrious and productive—a drive that involves self-perpetuating "ongoing activity" *(Be-trieb)*.

As Heidegger argues, scientific research occurs most fully within the institution of the university, which, as its name suggests, claims as its domain of research the universe as a whole. As such, scientific research extends from the physical sciences into the developing (during the 1930s) social sciences and even into the human sciences. A "scientific" form of history, for example (as exemplified by nineteenth-century historiography), is understood as the objective depiction of the past as a series of present moments that are causally joined to one another. Those presences—periods, events, and people—are then investigated in detail as the "cultural heritage" that is transmitted from the past age to the current age through the communicational medium of culture and time.

According to Heidegger, the essence of science consists in picturing the earth and the universe as worlds set before us. Scientific knowledge is a re-presentation of society and nature, a knowledge that is authorized as true through the precedence and the mediation of scientific method. Through scientific research, the world, and even man within it, is thought in terms of its being information—that is, in terms of its being objectively present-at-hand *(vorhanden)* for man's comprehension, management, and use. Thus, for modern science, all true beings and events are not only present in terms of their re-presentation but, according to the cultural logic of science, *can and should be represented and made available for management and use.* As such, all beings are understood in terms of the "experience" and possible experience of man, made present through the media of technical reproduction. All of life becomes, for modern man, matter for his "life-experience" *(Erlebnis)*[3]—an "experience" of "life" and objects at an objective, contemplative distance (134). And all beings are judged in terms of their "value" within this context of man's life-experience (141). The knowing subject of "man" thus becomes the measure for beings as a whole.

For Heidegger, Otlet's vision of the world as pictured on a private screen is the exact image of the increasing aesthetic distance and the collapsed spatial and temporal distance that is brought about through technical reproduction. The correspondence between Otlet's vision of history and the future and Heidegger's characterization of metaphysics and scientific modernity could not be more exact—and more opposed in terms of these two authors' claims regarding historical and social value. For Otlet, his vision of technological determinism *is* history, whereas for Heidegger, this type of historical vision is the imposition of metaphysics and positive science upon the occurrence of history itself.

Heidegger's 1938 lecture concludes with the prediction that because modernity understands the world in terms of representation, the future unfolding of modern history will involve conflicts between the most deterministic and extreme "world views," that is, between cultures that have most industrialized and acculturated themselves according to the logic of the world picture. Heidegger, in anticipation of World War II and the Cold War, writes:

> In such producing, man contends for the position in which he can be that particular being who gives the measure and draws up the guidelines for everything that is. Because this position secures, organizes, and articulates itself as a world view, the modern relationship to that which is, is one that becomes, in its decisive unfolding, a confrontation of world views; and indeed, not of random world views, but only of those that have already taken up the fundamental position of man that is most extreme, and have done so with utmost resoluteness. For the sake of this struggle of world views and in keeping with its meaning, man brings into play his unlimited

power for the calculating, planning, and molding of all things. Science as research is an absolutely necessary form of this establishing of self in the world; it is one of the pathways upon which the modern age rages toward fulfillment of its essence, with a velocity unknown to the participants. With this struggle of world views the modern age first enters into the part of its history that is the most decisive and probably the most capable of enduring. (134–35)

The themes in "The Age of the World Picture" narrated above continue to be repeated and developed in Heidegger's more philosophically technical works after the end of World War II and throughout the Cold War. In "The Question Concerning Technology," for example, modern technology is discussed in terms of a positive scientific framing and bringing to presence *(Ge-stell)* that understands beings as not only objective things *(Gegenstand)* but as things that are ordered forth *(Be-stellen)* so as to present themselves to man as a "standing-reserve" of resources *(Be-stand)*. Heidegger uses the examples of a field of coal and of the Rhine River insofar as both are understood in terms of being resources for energy. Human beings are also taken as a man-aged resource, for example, in the case of hospital and health care management: "The current talk about human resources, about the supply of patients to a clinic . . ." *("Die umlaufende Rede vom Menschenmaterial, vom Krankenmaterial einer Klinik . . .")* (18). For Heidegger in this essay, even theoretical physics, though it conceives of nature in terms other than that of traditional physics, remains part of the metaphysical tradition that understands that "nature reports itself in some way or other that is identifiable through calculation and . . . remains orderable as a system of information" *("dass sich die Natur in irgendeiner rechnerisch feststellbaren Weise meldet und als ein System von Informationen bestellbar bleibt")* (23).

In his 1959 lecture, "The Way to Language," Heidegger discusses the manner by which scientific-technical understanding turns language into a device for informing—a transformation that transforms humans into elements within a scientific-technical system of being and knowledge. Humans are "in-formed" by the form of the scientific-technical understanding of language that inhabits information or communication theory:

> Within Framing, speaking turns into information *[Das so gestellte Sprechen wird zur Information]*. It informs itself about itself in order to safeguard its own procedures

by information theories. Framing—the nature of modern technology holding sway in all directions—commandeers for its purposes a formalized language, the kind of communication which "informs" man uniformly, that is, gives him the form in which he is fitted into the technological-calculative universe and gradually abandons "natural language." . . . Information theory conceives of the natural aspect of language as a lack of formalization [*Die Informationstheorie begreift das Natürliche als den Mangel an Formalisierung*]. (132)

For Heidegger, even as late as his essay "The End of Philosophy and the Task of Thinking," the metaphysics of science as presence—understood in terms of "information" and information theory and most lately in terms of cybernetics—not only threatens to absorb knowledge and scholarship, physical objects, human subjects, and history but also appears now destined to determine even the very nature of language, the form that the future may take, and the meaning of previously resistant or critical forms of knowledge such as art:

> No prophecy is necessary to recognize that the sciences now establishing themselves will soon be determined and steered by the new fundamental science which is called cybernetics.
>
> This science corresponds to the determination of man as an acting social being. For it is the theory of the steering of the possible planning and arrangement of human labor. Cybernetics transforms language into an exchange of news. The arts become regulated-regulating instruments of information. (376)

In his 1961 lecture, "Kant's Thesis about Being," Heidegger bitterly jokes that it is becoming increasingly difficult to address the topic of this lecture, since it is becoming increasingly difficult in the context of the current mode of research in particular, and in the context of contemporary culture in general, to think about both Kant and ontology in critical relation to the Western metaphysical tradition. The difficulty Heidegger points to lies neither in Kant's philosophy nor in the problem of being. Rather, the difficulty lies with the way "scientific" scholarship demands that these questions be posed and studied. For, inasmuch as an encounter with the metaphysical tradition is mediated by such scholarship, this "scholarship" demands that it is "the job of the thinker to furnish information *[Auskunft]* about what is called 'being'" (337). For Heidegger, such a positivist demand immediately forecloses the critical thinking of being by framing that thinking within the determination of traditional Western metaphysics, namely, in terms of opposition and representation. This demand that Kant and ontology be thought of in terms of opposition and representation immediately undoes a more genuine and useful encounter with Kant's work and the ontological tradition, much less with the question of being itself. Heidegger comments that perhaps this cultural demand to think "objectively" about being is even too much for any thinker.

Heidegger's work throughout his lifetime argued that a critical form of philosophical thinking that takes as its task the analytical "destruction" *(Being and Time)* of metaphysics is a type of thinking that must begin with the very aporias posed by that tradition, going back to its foundational origins in ancient Greek and Latin philosophy. For Heidegger, quantitative calculation, operationalism, and instrumentality are intrinsic to metaphysics as it develops from the Latin appropriation of ancient Greek philosophy and culture[4] to its essence in the historical unfolding of the modern era, particularly in the forms of modern science and the ideologies of information and communication. A genuine critical encounter with the metaphysical tradition cannot take place, therefore, through a positivist epistemology and method that is thoroughly defined by the metaphysical tradition. And since nineteenth- and twentieth-century historiography assumes its form from this tradition's epistemology, the questioning of the history and social value of modern technology *first of all involves the questioning of that historiography and the futuristic projections that arise out of it.*

From the perspective of a dominant metaphysics or ideology, Otlet was absolutely *correct* in his understanding of history according to technological determinism. Where Otlet was utterly *wrong,* however, was in not critically thinking about that historiography and the tragic historical and social implications of his assumptions. In other words, Otlet's discourse demonstrated a failure to read history and social events in any sort of reflexive critical manner and thus demonstrated a model of historicity that tended toward political co-optation rather than toward the type of political responsibility Otlet so highly valued. Otlet's reading of history merely followed a narrative of technical progress that was the product of dominant social powers. A naive historiography worked in tandem with a naive sense of politics to the point where Otlet's "liberal" prognoses converged with totalitarian practices.

Heidegger's social criticism of technology develops out of his critique of the metaphysical tradition. Heidegger's critique of science and technology is part of his critique of the Western philosophical tradition's conception of being and truth. Inasmuch as Heidegger's writings critique the notion of technically determined representations of being and beings, they remain relevant to this day in the discussion of such phenomena as the "global," the "information society," the "information age," and the dominance of "information" and "communication" within knowledge and society.

As I have suggested, Heidegger's critique of technical reproduction develops out of not only a philosophical context but also a social one. It understands information and communication within the context of Western metaphysics and science and in terms of modern industrialism. Its critical advantage lies in its skeptical view regarding the assignment of truth to beings in representation.

Whereas Heidegger investigated Western culture through a critique of representation, documentation understood the culmination and salvation of "mankind" in terms of the systematization of forms of representation into a global totality. For Heidegger, truth lay in the event of revealing, which reveals most of all man's problematic relationship to being. In contrast, for documentation as a science, the event of truth must be mediated by a consistency in reproductive method, technique, and technology so that meaning resides not in the event but in the outcome of systematic production, that is, in the representational product or "object." Documentary truth lay in the correspondence between the world and its picture.

Social theorist Walter Benjamin's later work constitutes an extended materialist critical intervention into this production and systematization of representation, insofar as Benjamin reads this historical project in terms of "bourgeois history"—a history dominated by a narrative myth of progress overlaid upon the reality and contradictions of material production. Whereas Heidegger sought truth in the hermeneutics of being, Benjamin's analysis of the reification or fetishism of beings, objects, and events constitutes a critique of modern capitalism and its production of hegemony through mass communication and information. For Benjamin, "information" and "communication," as well as a historical reading of these words in terms of modern progress, must be subjected to counterreadings grounded in questioning their historical origins in material production. According to this critique, such rhetoric as that which surrounds Lévy's the "virtual," for example, must be read according to its cultural "aura," that is, in terms of its inflated claims and the social conditions that demand and support its production and stability.

Walter Benjamin and the Object of History

In what follows, I focus on five essays and the fragments of Walter Benjamin's larger Paris Arcades Project, a collection of notes and other materials from the late 1920s to early 1940, in order to give a picture of Benjamin's engagement with the congruence of aesthetics, history, knowledge, and technical reproduction in the modern phenomena of public information. These texts are "The Author as Producer" (1934), "The Work of Art in the Age of Mechanical Reproduction" ("Das Kunstwerk im Zeitalter seiner technischen Reproduzierbarkeit") (1935), "Paris, the Capital of the Nineteenth Century" (1935), "On Some Motifs in Baudelaire" (1939), and "Theses on the Philosophy of History" (1940). The ideas in these essays are developed out of the Arcades Project,[5] which itself dates from 1927 until Benjamin's death in 1940 (subsequently collected in Benjamin's *Gesammelte Schriften* under the title *Das Passagen-Werk*). My focus will be on that section of *Das Passagen-Werk* known as "Konvolut 'N,'" a section that centers upon epistemological issues and problems in the philosophy of history *(Geschichtsphilosophie)*. In that section, Benjamin outlines a critique of a certain type of philosophy of history and historiographical method that he terms "historicism"—that is, a "bourgeois" theory of history based on bourgeois myths of industrial progress and bourgeois strategies of cultural reification.

As "The Work of Art in the Age of Mechanical Reproduction" and "On Some Motifs in Baudelaire" argue, the nineteenth century was witness to an alienation and bifurcation of personal and social being through the impact or "shock" of technical reproduction. For Benjamin, the shock of industrial modernity upon "tradition" gave rise to both a technological optimism and a technological utopianism (for example, Saint-Simonism) as well as to an "atrophy of experience" *("Die Verkummerung der Erfahrung")*. Further, for Benjamin, this "atrophy of experience" involved a bifurcation of experience into an "inner sense" of experience (a new, "personalized" sense of *Erfahrung*) and into a sense of experience as something "publicly" lived through *(Erlebnis)* ("On Some Motifs in Baudelaire" 159). The difference between "experience" in terms of *Erfahrung* and of *Erlebnis* is important, because it indicates a split in the subject between private and public "selves" and spaces as well as a decrease in the importance of what we now might term the "local" or "personal" experience as a measure for "public" meaning and social fact.

Experience as *Erlebnis* is exemplified for Benjamin in newspapers, where news becomes a form of knowledge that stands at a distance from a more unified notion of experience. It has this status due to both professional and rhetorical requirements ("freshness of the news, brevity, comprehensibility, and above all, lack of connection between the individual new items" ["On Some Motifs in Baudelaire" 158–59]) and to its need for mass circulation. The "public" distance that modern newspapers introduce into experience by presenting experience in terms of public information is, for Benjamin, both a symptom and a continuation of the effect of modernist shock. The generalized and fragmented nature of modern journalism is, in other words, an attempt to control violence in modern life—violence that exceeds the capacity of traditional narratives rooted in localized and traditional contexts and that has already shattered these contexts and replaced them with mass industrialization, the modern city, and mass culture. For Benjamin, public information in such forms as newspaper stories acts as a form of "shock defense." The generalized information of the news media, for example, constitutes the farthest distance through which shocks in modern life can be experienced so that their violence is negated within general forms of knowledge that are applicable to no particular person:

> Newspapers constitute one of many evidences of such an inability [of a modern human being to "assimilate the data of the world around him by way of experience"]. If it were the intention of the press to have the reader assimilate the information it supplies as part of his own experience, it would not achieve its purpose. But its intention is just the opposite, and it is achieved: to isolate what happens from the realm in which it could affect the experience of the reader. . . . Perhaps the special achievement of shock defense may be seen in its function of assigning to an incident a precise point in time in consciousness at the cost of the integrity of its contents. This would be a peak achievement in the intellect; it would turn the incident into a moment that has been lived *(Erlebnis)* [versus one that has been personally experienced in the mode of *Erfahrung*]. ("On Some Motifs in Baudelaire" 158–63)

For Benjamin, mass-circulated public information, first in the form of newspapers, then radio, and finally film, separates the reported or depicted experience from local senses of tradition in which the individual's experiences once found cohesion ("where there is experience *[Erfahrung]* in the strict sense of the word, certain contents of the individual past combine with material of the collective past" ["On Some Motifs in Baudelaire"

159]). In this same essay, Benjamin suggests that Freud's understanding of war trauma (the repetition of a traumatic war event within dreams as an attempt to get hold of the event at a safe mental distance) analogously explains the need for shock in cinema and film—it is trauma made safe through its dramatic repetition:

> Thus technology has subjected the human sensorium to a complex kind of training. There came a day when a new and urgent need for stimuli was met by the film. In a film, perception in the form of shocks [as an individual experiences while being jostled within a crowd or while acting as the receptor to mechanical affects when working on an assembly line] was established as a formal principle. That which determines the rhythm of production on a conveyor belt is the basis of the rhythm of reception in film.[6] (175)

According to Benjamin, nineteenth-century technical reproduction created this bifurcation of experience by plunging individuals into the anonymous crowds of industrial cities and into gigantic markets where mass-produced goods were sold, forever divorced from their sources of production. It also created this bifurcation by incorporating people within anonymous and repetitive industrial labor. Both the crowd of consumption and the incorporation of the individual within in its production are reproduced in public information. For Benjamin, the critical question is how to create a narrative form that can respond to modernist shock without seeking solace in the universal anonymity of traditional journalism, reportage, and the formal techniques of representation and aesthetic mimesis. For Benjamin, it is impossible not to respond to the shock of modernity: technical reproduction in the form of mass production and consumption cannot be escaped from. Localized and unified histories (tradition), art (in the form of rituals of interpretation, forming what Benjamin calls the "aura" of the traditional art work), and older forms of knowledge and experience are shattered by material and social mechanization and the resulting phenomena of simultaneous crowd formations and psychological isolation. Out of these various forms of shock, claims Benjamin in "On Some Motifs in Baudelaire," come the self-narrating tendencies found in Baudelaire's poetry, the narration of the self in Proust's reconstruction of memory, and the sense of a recoverable unconscious in Freud, as well as the more "objective" narrative forms found in the mass media. In other words, the subjective "self," as well as the objective "fact," are results of the insertion of industrial shock into traditional societies, a phenomenon that shattered the relationship between labor and meaning. The *critical* question in Benjamin's work is how not to have a writing and art form that is simply a reactive symptom to the shock of modernity and thus how not to produce both a writer and reader (viewer, listener, and so on) who is simply a symptom of that modernity as well.

This is a critical question for Benjamin because it attempts to create a distance in relation to modernity even as it takes place within and through modernity. Such a question turns Benjamin toward avant-garde art forms that assume a critical relationship toward modern culture while using the very devices and objects that are the essence of modernity (for example, shock effects from mass-produced objects, language, and images, as well as the technique of aesthetic distance). Such practices and forms constitute the avant-garde tradition of the Soviet and European formalists, constructivists, and futurists, as well as the dadaists and even the surrealists. Benjamin turns to such traditions in search of a critical and formal engagement that not only would allow a critique of normative or "bourgeois" representation but would also construct a manner of presentation that could engage those elements of reality that were remaindered by technical reproduction. For Benjamin, his historiography could accomplish its mission if it did not simply reproduce or oppose technical reproduction but instead intervened at the level of the object's commoditization or, conversely, its historical obscurity. Just as the artistic avant-garde desired to critically engage social production at the level of material production, so Benjamin desired to critically engage historical production at the level of the production of the popular image.

For Benjamin, a critical engagement with modern culture is an urgent task because politics formally organizes the individual's response to shock by means of social reification and the organization of mass groups and movements. With shock and the disintegration of localized traditions, both the mass and the individual appear. This bifurcation is real for Benjamin, but leaving it as a bifurcation fails to account for the force of industrial production in creating this division. The notion of "mass," for example, needs to be accounted for in terms of technical production, just as the individual is accounted for in terms of a remainder within industrial labor.

For Benjamin, the relation of these two forms of "mass"—that of the human crowd and that of technically reproduced objects and knowledge—is a political relation. As Benjamin's "Work of Art in the Age of Mechanical Reproduction" makes clear, fascism is characterized by "the introduction of aesthetics into political life" (241). The introduction of an aesthetics of reproduction and re-presentation into the social realm means the organization of everyday life based on these principles. Through aesthetics, and not simply as production, cultural life is normalized according to the "mass." Mass reproduction and representation become the normative "aura," not only of things, but also of individuals and groups.

Following the shattering of aura in preindustrialized society, fascism, for Benjamin, attempts to reorganize the scattered symbols of religion, local tradition, and labor so as to refound community through the State's newly organized "picture" of itself, a picture that claims to bring all the shattered pieces together toward "common" national goals. For Benjamin, fascism attains its innate promise in the raising up of "mankind" to the level of being a self-contemplative, speculative image (for example, within a political rally or as a nationalized people at war). Inasmuch as a human being can then contemplate himself or herself as a unity, "its self-alienation has reached such a degree that it can experience its own destruction as an aesthetic pleasure of the first order" ("Work of Art" 242).[7]

In response to politics' reorganization of life according to an aesthetics of representation and reification (or fetish), "communism responds by politicizing art" (242). This is to say that communism responds to capitalism's reification of value by subjecting reified and commodified values to the objective, contradictory, and disparate experiences of everyday life for the "masses" under capitalist production, as revealed through critical and defamiliarizing techniques in the arts. For Benjamin in Western Europe in the 1930s, an encounter with fascism's political (re)organization of the "masses" as a national aura or commodity could be met only by a critique of that political-aesthetic strategy through an analytical "destruction" of it, created by reproductive technologies and techniques whose effects were not yet fully ideologically organized or "aura-ized." Only by holding open processes of technical reproduction, instead of closing such reproduction up in the aura of the commodity or spectacle, could critique take place at the level of the masses. Thus, for this *political* reason, Benjamin critically reopens the problem of the relation of technical reproduction to aesthetic form in the construction of personal being and community.

Benjamin, in his 1934 lecture to the Paris Institute for the Study of Fascism, "The Author as Producer," for example, drew upon a formalist understanding of art and knowledge production that reached back to his interests in the dadaists' and Soviet avant-garde's use of montage. By the 1930s, Benjamin's knowledge of the Soviet avant-garde was largely through film, literature, photography, and, most of all, the close personal relationship that he had formed with the German avant-garde writer and playwright Bertolt Brecht, whose own theory and practice of theater and literature was strongly influenced—through both personal acquaintance and cultural knowledge—by the Soviet avant-garde.[8]

For Benjamin, in the context of these politically left, formalist avant-garde arts, the arts are "progressive" only inasmuch as they utilize fragments of material reality in manners that disrupt the political construction of a mass or national aura upon objects and open those materials to utilization by viewers and readers. A prime example of this type of interruption occurs in the work of photography, and further in photomontage, when, respectively, objects and actions are photographically presented (destroying the traditional rituals of interpretation that the painter's artwork depended on to hold the viewer's attention and to situate the meaning of the work) and then that material is itself subjected to montage techniques in photomontage in order to break whatever ideological forces may be operating in the attempt to reconstitute aura on the photograph. Photography was a noteworthy technology for Benjamin, not so much because it "realistically" depicted the object but rather because it broke the aura of cultural, social, and political framing that was so crucial for painting. In turn, however, it was the purpose of the dadaist use of photographs and other materials to break, among other "frames" or auras, that of photorealism by means of the juxtaposition of "intrusive" cultural materials. Benjamin's argument in this case is that each new technology of reproduction brings with it the ability to smash the commoditization of values that the preceding technologies have been inscribed with. The opening of such technologies to use value, instead of to commodity value, is a temporary but important opening insofar as it opens up the ideological frame around the signification of objects. After photography, dada was important insofar as it restated the primacy of the object in art against representational aesthetics:

> The revolutionary strength of Dadaism consisted in testing art for its authenticity. Still lifes put together from tickets, spools of cotton, cigarette butts, that were linked with painted elements. The whole thing was put in a frame. And thereby the public was shown: look, your picture frame ruptures time; the tiniest authentic fragment of daily life says more than painting. ("Author as Producer" 229)

As Benjamin argues in his commentary on Brecht's theater in "The Author as Producer," art is valuable only in its "interruption" of an illusion of "reality" by the montage of disparate social materials. Inasmuch as art breaks ideological frames or "auras," it produces gaps in lived experience *(Erlebnis)* through which "situations" *(Zustände)* appear to the viewer in moments of "astonishment" *(Staunen).* The shattering of illusion and the emergence of the conditions of production in everyday life through moments of historical recognition are the political goals that pit art against public information, montage against realism, and historical materialism against capitalist reification.

For Benjamin, the importance of technical reproduction in the production of social meaning lies in its ability to utilize materials in a technical fashion so that the producer's first responsibility would be toward problems of material construction rather than aesthetic form and aesthetic appreciation. Technical production within a communist approach, for example, would involve approaching "information" from the aspect of its social and material construction rather than from the aspect of its reified value as an empirical fact. Knowledge could be gleamed from the public information of the bourgeois mass media but only insomuch as its images and the media itself were subject to critical technique. Bourgeois information was, for example, dialectically objectified as material for early Soviet and dadaist montage; its realism was stripped from it for revolutionary means.

For Benjamin, film embodied one of the most progressive forms for montage in that it both photographed "reality" and yet technically dissected that reality and reconstructed it by means of cutting and splicing, slowing and speeding up action, closing in and widening perspectives. Film, for Benjamin, is inherently linked to mass social formation because of its need to recuperate its cost of production through mass distribution. In Benjamin's "Work of Art in the Age of Mechanical Reproduction," filmmakers such as Dziga Vertov (one of the most famous of the early Soviet avant-garde filmmakers) and Charlie Chaplin (presumably because of his comedic distancing of capitalist and fascist myths about production and about the State) are favored by Benjamin. For Benjamin, revolutionary film took the rhythmical shock of modernist perception and created a counterrhythm out of it and against it. The most promising film is one whose rhythm does not simply duplicate the rhythm of modernity but also disrupts it toward what Benjamin calls a "moment of recognizability." This "moment of recognizability" is embodied in the existence of production as remainder—namely, the remainder of the human worker and his or her material reality.

Benjamin's own writing attempted to approach this standard for a politically responsible sense of historicity inasmuch as it took as its starting point a critical reading of modern history and bourgeois historicism and historiography. As Benjamin notes in one of the passages in *The Arcades Project,* section "N," "The first stage in this undertaking [of writing about the Paris arcades] will be to carry over the principle of montage into history" ([N2,6] 461).[9] In contrast to the bourgeois dream of modern history as progress, Benjamin argues that "materialist historiography . . . is based on a constructive principle. Thinking involves not only the flow of thoughts, but their arrest as well" ("Theses on the Philosophy of History" 262).

For Benjamin, the importance of arresting the movement of bourgeois history lies in the revolutionary attempt to arrest and reveal the historical contradictions and antagonisms that are taken up and canceled by a narrative of progress. With "progress," the social dialectics or antagonisms that make up history are overcome and canceled, and dialectical materialism turns into historical speculation and utopianism. The critical arrest of historicism, on the other hand, interrupts its utopian movement, exposing the material conditions for meaning.

For Benjamin, one manner of accomplishing this arrest is to reinsert materials that have been left as historical remainders outside the narrative frame of progress. Reinserting the "remainders" *(Abfall)*[10] of history as material, such as the defunct Paris arcades, but also men and women in their everyday lives,[11] historical/historiographic interruption locks up progress's subsumption of history through a sort of return of the material repressed. Modernist dialectic as a subsuming process is brought to a standstill, exposing an ambiguity or antagonism within certain images of existence. As Benjamin writes in his *Arcades* exposé of 1935:

> Ambiguity is the manifest imaging of dialectic, the law of dialectics at a standstill. This standstill is utopia and the dialectical image, therefore, dream image. Such an image is afforded by the commodity per se: as fetish. Such an image is presented by the arcades, which are house no less than street. Such an image is the prostitute—seller and sold in one. (*Arcades Project* 10)

If the commodity as fetish speaks of a dream state that masks the reality of industrial culture, and if it is the function of a bourgeois understanding of history to continue this dream state through the hegemony of its discourses, institutions, and historiographies across cultural space, then it is the function of a critical, materialist history to interrupt this dream, its appearance, and its ideological propagation by a form of historical dream interpretation ([N4,1] 464) and a subsequent moment of historical "awak-ening." In the "now" *(Jetztzeit)* of this awakening, the dialectic of bour-geois history is brought to a momentary standstill.[12] The house reappears from the arcades' street market. The commoditization of the prostitute reappears alongside her entrepreneurship. The remainders of life haunt an ideal narrative of commodity exchange, money, and everyday business. For Benjamin, the materialist historian approaches such a subject "only where he encounters it as a monad" ("Theses on the Philosophy of History" 263). In the dialectical standstill of the monadic bourgeois image, historical narratives leading up to this image and leading out of it are caught in a momentary "freeze."

Technical reproduction or representation is not the central issue here—Brecht's stage depictions, for example, were quite "real" for Benjamin; they were not simulacra. The issue at hand is that of the aesthetic and ideologi-cal construction and repetition of the *meaning* of the technically produced image or event. The freezing of the dialectical image in its historical pro-gression was, for Benjamin, like a snapshot: in it, the objects of bourgeois history would fall out as residue from their historical flow. Benjamin was critical of ideologically driven repetition and consequent reification; tech-nical reproduction might be brought into its service, but it could also serve to break up aura by repeating or distorting the ideological image to the point of exhausting it back to an object status (Warhol would later utilize a similar strategy of informational exhaustion in his silk screens). Ideologi-cal meaning was the creation of a historical aura or frame through which objects were inscribed with certain meanings. Against aesthetic represen-tation, and with it, public information, the task of the materialist histo-rian and social critic, as well as the artist, was to break open this represen-tation, sometimes by means of technical reproduction.

For Benjamin, as was the case with art critiques, critically exercising a materialist historiography means "rescuing" the specificities and contra-dictions that compose life under capitalism from the bourgeois narratives of "progress" and "heritage." Materialist historiography is an attempt both to prevent the narration of beings in terms of their being informational elements in historicism and to "blast" objects out of such narratives and to recover their particular historical specificity, complexities, and agency. It is, thus, a critical intervention into a living idealized history of the past, present, and even the future:

> What are phenomena rescued from? Not only, and not
> in the main, from the discredit and neglect into which

they have fallen, but from the catastrophe represented very often by a certain strain in their dissemination, their "enshrinement as heritage."—They are saved through the exhibition of the fissure within them.—There is a tradition that is catastrophe. (*Arcades Project* [N9,4] 473)

The concept of progress must be grounded in the idea of catastrophe. That things are "status quo" *is* the catastrophe. ([N9a,1] 473)

If such media and forms of "information" as newspapers and historiographical "historicism" depict experience by neutralizing the violence and ruptures that mark everyday and historical modernity, Benjamin attempts to read that violence and those ruptures back into fetished knowledge, that is, back into information, demonstrating the forces of power and reification that construct the bourgeois construction of information. Inasmuch as early-twentieth-century information culture depended upon an informational form of historiography in order to construct the past, present, and, most important, the future, Benjamin's critical reading attempts to return the play of political forces to the meaning of historical objects. The intention of Benjamin's Arcades Project was to read social force and the pain of labor back into the crystal dream structures of the nineteenth-century marketplace.

If I could be excused in engaging in a bit of historicism for a moment, I might propose the following concluding image of the forces, people, and destinies that swirled around the construction of a culture of information before World War II. However fanciful, this image is based on a remarkable factual congruence of persons and places just before the full outbreak of that war.

Imagine the following: Walter Benjamin, a cultural critic of modernity, working toward the task of critically rupturing historiographies of technological and social progress that are leading capitalist and fascist countries into mass technological warfare, spends much of his last six years in exile (1934–40)—as a known Jewish, Marxist cultural critic from Germany—in the Bibliothèque Nationale researching his Paris Arcades Project. In the Bibliothèque Nationale, Benjamin utilizes both the graphic and written artifacts that the library houses and, as a resource, Georges Bataille, who had been active in his own battles against fascism through his critical and literary writings and through the Paris-based "College of Sociology" and who, as a librarian at the Bibliothèque Nationale, would save through the war years Benjamin's Arcades Project. As a researcher, Benjamin would also have most certainly utilized the Salle des Catalogues et des Bibliographies in order to find information for his project. In charge of the Salle des Catalogues is a librarian, a bit younger than Benjamin, a Madame Suzanne Briet, who would later carry on some of Otlet's ideas as vice president of the International Federation for Documentation and who would acquire the nickname "Madame Documentation." (Briet would later, in her autobiography, acknowledge Bataille's presence at the Bibliothèque Nationale by describing his blue eyes and burning heart but added at the end what an English reader at the library once said to her about him: "Good-looking boys know nothing" [English in the original; *Entre Aisne et Meuse . . . et au-delà: souvenirs* 121].) After the war, Briet would advocate in her manifesto, *Qu'est-ce que la documentation?*, such ideas as the cyborg integration of human beings and machine technologies and the technical and "cultural necessity" of "scientific" information management, systematicity, and standards, since, for Briet, documentation is a "cultural technique," and "our" culture is one of "science" that needs to be spread globally to developing countries (that is, former Western colonies). Briet's resurrection of information culture from its submersion in the military industrial machinery of World War II would be only partially successful on a historical scale; a more total theoretical integration of human agency within mechanical and social engineering would occur during the Cold War across the Atlantic with the Macy cybernetics conferences, and against this cultural "success," Briet and, indeed, the history of European documentation would be largely forgotten. Benjamin, on the other hand, wouldn't even live to see any of these events, because his image disappears off the map in 1940 as he apparently commits suicide while blocked from crossing the border into Spain in an unsuccessful attempt to flee Nazism and eventually reach the United States. Not until almost thirty years later would Benjamin's writings be more fully recovered in the English-speaking world. As a social critic and, even worse, as a communist, his information was nearly erased, especially in the United States, during the Cold War. His information—and history—was thought not to be relevant to an information culture or to social policy during those years, and perhaps this is true even now.

6 ▪ Conclusion: "Information" and the Role of Critical Theory

In this book, I have examined professional and authoritative texts that have attempted to valorize information and communication as central social values and that have attempted to reify such values in terms of modernist notions of progress, capitalist exchange value, and transcendental historicism. I have also given two examples of writers who were critical of these attempts, each in their different ways opposing a reduction of knowledge, history, affect, and language to reified notions of information and communication.

The problematic of information in our age is one that simultaneously involves aesthetic, ethical, and political values. These values are aspects of the relationship of affect and knowledge to social space, a relationship that generates historical forms and temporal events.

The problem of information is an aesthetic problem (broadly understood—in terms of both affective senses and art) because we become informed through a variety of senses and forms. As seen throughout this book, the meaning of "information" has recently come to be attributed with the characteristics of "factuality" and auto-affective presence. Within a technical theory of information or communication, these positive characterizations make a certain degree of sense since technological systems, at least when they are being engineered, can be rather well described and their parts and actions operationally defined in causal relation to one another. Causal *effect,* however, is not the same as sensory, emotive, or cognitive *affect.* The functioning and production of "information" in social space, as well as the appearance of what we might call information in so-called mental states, is neither strictly causal nor easily described in operational terms. Semiotic signs, including in "language" proper, are anything but obvious and fixed as to their meanings and values unless a great degree of context, contingency, and continuity are brought to bear upon them. This is to say that in order to gain the type of clear and distinct presence that is usually attributed to information, an extraordinary amount of control must be forced upon the sensory or cognitive process—either by tightly framing the object for perception or by habituating the subject toward a perception. Wiener recognized this need and the limitations upon mechanical design to achieve this. Since machines have innate limits in design for the purposes of cognitive adjustment, over the long run system design must work upon users. Communication, as Wiener understood it, necessitates control over human actors and communities in terms of standardizing semiotic affects and behavioral options.

The belief that such "aesthetic" or formal sensory or cognitive habituation for achieving a certain type of communication or information is desirable, however, must be questioned in a way that it is usually not in the positive social sciences or in policy studies that follow their techniques. One reason for this neglect may be that the positive social sciences themselves assume formal grounds in order to operationalize their subjects in terms of quantitative techniques and methods. But whereas in an idealized "science" of the social these formal grounds may appear as mere technical controls, in social space they are cultural, social, and political constructions of taste and action, or, simply put, they are ideology. The avoidance of the aesthetic or formal nature of "information" or "communication" is an avoidance of ideology and power as it operates upon agency through standardization and through the aesthetic construction of knowledge and social space by techniques of representation.

Given the manner through which "information" and "communication" are relegated to the positive social sciences and given the lack of tools for discussing ideology in the public arena (especially in the United States, and particularly within the political dominance of global neo-liberalism), it is not surprising that these problems of sensory and cognitive "framing" and of social production in regard to information and communication are not very much engaged by professional organizations involved with directing information research. As dedicated as professional organizations may be to producing policy statements and guidelines on such issues as information literacy, freedom of information, computer ethics, equal access, and the like, the critical problems of what information is, how information has been culturally constructed and produced, and how an ideology of information and communication is then globally spread is low on their members' research agenda. To put this another way, information professionals and theorists question very little what information is, why it should be valued, or why it is an economic and social "good." The term "information" often plays the role of a reified token in various ideological language games; such questions as, "Why is it important to 'have' information?.," "What does it mean to be 'information literate'?.," "What is the nature of the 'information society'?.," or even "What are the specific characteristics of 'information technologies'?" are rarely, in any fundamental way, asked, at least with any social, political, and historical depth. From the trope of information, other tropes are generated, forming a discourse of information (such as the "information society" and the infamous "information super-highway," as well as "information designers," "information architects," "information planners," and "ontologists" [formerly referred to as "catalogers"]). Indeed, the generation and maintenance of tropes surrounding that of information seems to constitute a profession unto itself.

Part of the problem, as I have suggested, involves method, and part of it involves the historically close relationship that often exists between professional institutions and discourses and dominant social and political institutions and discourses. In terms of method, quantitative methods—because of their focus upon a predefined "content" and not upon form—are rather poor at asking foundational questions, and even when they do ask such questions their vocabulary tends not to be very well developed for posing questions in a critical manner. Following the tradition of critical theory, I use "critical" here to mean that the standard manner and names for representing the issues at hand are disrupted by foundational, reflexive questions.[1] If theory is the construction of concepts, then critical theory is the deployment of concepts in critical and interruptive relation to the conceptual foundations of commonly accepted practices. Heidegger's fear about the lack of critical thought in modern research and professional organizations is, I believe, very relevant to today's research on information, as well as to other topics. Once a representational framing or *reissen* has occurred—particularly if it speculates upon military or economic gains—it is practically impossible for it to close up again. (Artificial Intelligence or the Strategic Defense Initiative are two nice examples of research areas where research streams are very little hindered by either critical doubts or empirical failures.) The unwillingness of research on information to actually attempt to situate a culture of information and communication in terms of interested and powerful social and historical forces is evident by even a brief glance at journals in information management or information studies or in policy papers. Coupled with the dominant tendency of such research to be "practical" in the service of professional and business organizations and in the service of military and industrial research projects, research in information simply shies away from critical engagement, as well as from foundational, qualitative, or materialist analyses, especially from that which is seen to employ "pretentious," "political," or, equally, "foreign" vocabulary, let alone philosophical or Marxist analyses. What is at stake here is not only the social production of a professional or scholarly field such as "information science" but ideological limitations upon concepts, vocabulary, and other practical tools for analyzing the cultural reality or nature of information and of the information society that we are repeatedly told that we are socially in and historically moving toward. Too often, the terms "practical," "science," (historical) "age," and others mask those ideological boundaries that block critical agency and thought from straying off standardized communicational and informational routes. "Information" is a central term of ideology because it determines and patrols its own meaning over a vast expanse of social and cultural spaces. Through information, vocabularies for the future are included or excluded, shaping history in a way that is fit for information and for little else.

The world of information that we are given by foundational texts and traditions of information in the twentieth century is a deeply troubling and problematic one. It is troubling because of its seeming naturalness and common sensibility and because of the ease of its predications for an information age of the present and the future. It is problematic because its claims are far too simplistic and reductionistic of the complexities of sense, knowledge, and agency in the world and because a careful examination of its own claims and foundational models reveals vast and deep exclusions and contradictions. These qualities do not mean that certain dominant rhetorics about information are "wrong" but rather that a tradition of values for information has been established and has been, rather uncritically and ahistorically, promulgated as a "good" not only for Western culture but, more troubling, for, and as, "the global."

The point here is not to suggest what information "really is" or is not, nor is it to suggest that information is "good" or "bad," but rather that certain connotations of information, and the cultural and social privileging of certain technologies and techniques associated with it, are cultural and social productions that elevate certain values over other values and have doomed certain historical events and critiques to oblivion or near-oblivion. That a critical approach is rarely taken to the modern notion of information might suggest that the concept of information is not approachable in this manner. To the contrary, however, the lack of critical analysis is a function of power and ideology rather than any more neutral cause, and this can be shown by examining the rhetoric and history of information.

That such an analysis is rare, however, perhaps reveals that language, as well as history, is not very much an issue for the "information age" in any manner other than as a problem of transmission that can be solved. The "problem" of language, however, cannot be "solved" because it is not simply an object of study; rather, it constitutes the primary conditions through which study occurs. The same is true of "history." And the same may be said of certain other horizons of knowledge and sense that are reduced to being informational content in the information age. As Theodor Adorno wrote of his experiences at the Princeton Radio Project just before World War II, where he was asked to do "administrative research" on popular music, "A small machine which enabled a listener to indicate what he liked and didn't like by pushing a button during the performance of a piece of music appeared to be highly inadequate to the complexity of what had to be discovered" ("Scientific Experiences" 344). Just as Adorno found that the quantifiable, "informational" measure of cultural phenomenon was deeply problematic and itself ignored foundational conceptual, social, and political issues in order to serve ideologically defined "practical" goals, so too have I suggested in this book that an informational approach to information has produced a cultural history and philosophy of information that is far too simplistic and politically convenient.

The problem of the aesthetics of information—that is to say, the problem of knowledge as the paradox of "factual representation"—has, thus, a strong "ethical" component as well. (And by this term I mean more than a code of prescriptive or proscriptive moral values.) The critical ethical obligation is to bring both common "practical" actions and reified concepts and objects into question through an examination of their institutional, political, and social assumptions and to act out of reflexive relationships to material forces and production. And insofar as a critical ethics engages social, cultural, and epistemic foundations in order to bring their productions and codings into view, such an ethics itself then occupies a space where imperatives to act are decisions made neither in ignorance nor in certainty, where action is—in a sense familiar to Deleuze's, Derrida's, and Negri's writings—im-possible and must take its cue neither from guesses nor from ideal nor dictatorial systems but from reflexive relations with material conditions and historical context. A critical ethics does not have a transhistorical or moral sense from which to be certain, but instead, operating out of a critical relationship between such senses and material resistances to these senses, it attempts to articulate a historical presence that responds to material necessity, even as it must historically do so from a critical relation to the ideal. In brief, all critical ethics is founded in risk. It is founded through a reflexive relation with negative horizons that are specified by materiality and time. These dual limitations construct the category of necessity from which ethical thought and action issue. And this includes, of course, an ethical relationship to the politically and culturally charged notion of information.

Therefore, the political component of critical studies of information follows the critical aesthetic investigation and its ethical obligations and consequences. The politics that are suggested are, of course, those of an agency whose ethical obligation is to engage the very form or aesthetics of politics as it is promised and practiced in a social space defined by a normative concept of information. Thus, Benjamin's materialist critique engages a modernist speculative politics from the aspects of the remainders of ideological production. Benjamin's critical *respons-ibility* is both a destructive one toward exploitation and neglect made possible by ideology and reification and a constructive one that finds its empirical impetus from those materials that capital has either left behind or cannot symbolically recuperate into its own master narratives. In a world where respons-ibility and thus community are increasingly mediated by the presence and promise of the legal State, where value and conditions of value are determined by industrial powers, and where knowledge and conditions of knowledge are mediated by statistical information, critical interventions upon modernity are forms of risk that work against reified information and work from truly *material* information.

Thus, what I mean by "critical" obviously is not simply the product of criticism (in a moral or liberal sense); rather, this term marks an otherness to common sense that has found itself having first to question a large part of what is characterized as information and communication. Given this contrast and given the social and cultural dominance of positive thought, critical action may thus appear as totally "impractical," "impossible," and "theoretical." And in a sense, such a charge is totally true, but only if it is viewed from the realm of ideology itself. Theory and practice exist in opposition when practice is simply seen as the application of theory and theory is simply seen as the abstraction of practice. A theory and practice distinction exists only in terms of representation and an idealistic or positivist understanding of the relation of words and things, concepts and empirical facts. Contrary to this view, from the perspective of critical theory, "theory" is a form of practice when it engages the reification of the world as the practice of society and thought. Positivist thought cannot account for theory as a form of practice because it cannot account for empirical facts as social or linguistic constructs and, conversely, social or linguistic constructs as empirical facts.

I propose that information is different from knowledge (at least inasmuch as "knowledge" signifies, since the eighteenth century, analytical knowledge), but only if we take an opposing view to the trajectory of the term "information" in the twentieth century. Information is the quality of being informed. But this is a highly ambiguous—"theoretical" and affective—state of affairs, one that leaves the nature of knowledge, as well as of the world and the subject, still to be formed and discovered. And it is a sign of the times that such a simple but "risky" notion of information is not only evaded but also buried by a reified and commoditized notion of "information," for the "world" as a whole now seems to be once again wagered on an ideological rhetoric of information and its promise of a future.

Notes
Works Cited
Index

▪ Notes

2. European Documentation: Paul Otlet and Suzanne Briet

1. The most comprehensive work on Paul Otlet's work has been done by W. Boyd Rayward and Michael Buckland. Rayward has written the only complete biography of Otlet, *The Universe of Information: The Work of Paul Otlet for Documentation and International Organisation.* The secondary materials on Otlet and his work have been increasing in recent years. See, for example, the two special topic issues of the *Journal of the American Society for Information Science (JASIS)* on the history of documentation and information science (vol. 48, nos. 4 and 9 [April and September 1997]), reprinted in Hahn and Buckland.

2. The term "man," as often used in this book between quotation marks, refers to the philosophical concept or "question of man" that arose in the eighteenth century as a problem of natural classification, continuing the problem of the essence of man that arose in Renaissance humanism. From this historical context, it is impossible not to see that this question is both patriarchal in nature even as it is humanist. My examination of this concept in this book is an attempt to draw attention to both the gendered and the idealist biases and desires at work in the history of information. For more on the history of this term, especially in the context of the emergence of the human sciences, see Michel Foucault, *The Order of Things.*

3. For earlier German instances of the "monographic principle," see Hapke.

4. Otlet's neologism "bibliological" is sometimes used in his texts as a more general term than "bibliographical" for the study and "laws" of books, documentation, and other media. Otlet, however, often uses the terms as synonyms of one another, and in this book I will use the more traditional—and thus less confusing—term "bibliographical," even though Otlet's neologism is, perhaps, more descriptive and accurate of the range of his concerns.

5. For more on H. G. Wells's concept of the "world brain," see W. Boyd Rayward, "H. G. Wells's Idea of a World Brain"; for Ostwald's conception of the world brain *(Gehirn der Welt),* see Hapke.

6. Briet writes in her article "Bibliothécaires et Documentalistes" ("Librarians and Documentalists"): "The sciences and the technical fields are in need of rapid information, whereas the human sciences proceed through accumulation rather than by replacement" (43). Briet goes on to insist that despite this difference in methodology, the human sciences are in need of documentation as well because they are part of a cultural shift that demands documentation. The differences between the humanities and the sciences are so clear for Briet, however, that they help constitute the division between the functions of libraries and librarians and those of centers of documentation and documentalists. These two functions, for Briet, involve distinct cultures and require distinct attitudes and education. In this regard, it is interesting to note, too, Martin Heidegger's remarks in his

1938 lecture, "The Age of the World Picture," about the advent of the academic "researcher" and the demise of the "scholar" (125). That Heidegger characterizes this historical change by the absence of a personal library for the modern researcher curiously echoes documentation's desire to professionalize and systemize the bibliographical collection and research functions that the scholar had traditionally performed for himself or herself. In chapter 5, I will engage this section of Heidegger's text in more detail.

7. Briet is referring to Robert Pagès's article, "Transformations documentaires et milieu culturel (Essai de documentologie)." Pagès was a colleague from whom Briet borrowed many of her most important ideas. Unfortunately, very little biographical material exists on him.

8. For a discussion of Dewey's relationship to modernist notions of efficiency, bureaucratic management, and what would become known as Taylorism, see Casey.

9. Félix Guattari and Eric Alliez's essay, "Capitalistic Systems, Structures, and Processes," remains exceptional in its proposal that capitalist systems are essentially defined by the implantation of semiotic control within the social and personal body, thus encoding certain notions of value and desire within such bodies. Such an analysis, of course, has powerful implications for studies engaged with analyzing the relationship between information and communication systems on the one hand and social and psychological forms on the other during the Cold War and in the so-called postindustrial New World Order. The notion of "colonialism," here, of course, would take on the meaning of encoding not only national bodies but individual ones, not only social habits but psychological states.

3. Information Theory, Cybernetics, and the Discourse of "Man"

1. Some excellent critical literature exists on these conferences and on the relation of cybernetic theory to social and psychological theories (historical and contemporary). Foremost, see Paul N. Edwards's history of computers and Cold War culture, *The Closed World* (particularly chapters 6 and 7), and for an excellent reading of the relationship between cybernetics and psychiatric theory (particularly upon the establishment of panic disorder), see Jackie Orr's articles that are beginning to appear in the field of sociology.

2. Part of the skepticism that the participants in the Macy cybernetics conferences felt toward psychoanalytic contributions to the conferences (specifically, in the form of Lawrence Kubie's contributions) may be understood in terms of the inability for the psychoanalytic cure to be "permanent" and for the "war" on mental illness to be "winnable" by these means. In this specific historical example, the positivist zero-sum expectations that governed the cybernetic project can be seen as clashing with a romantic tradition of negativity and excess (here, through psychoanalysis's notion of the unconscious). In psychoanalysis, the "cure" to nonnormative behavior is never final because neurotic symptoms occur due to historical and social etiologies that establish themselves in individuals in ways that exceed operational control over time. Briefly put, the foundational models that psychoanalysis and cybernetics assume for subjectivity, language, mental states, and temporality are radically different from one another. For the history of psychoanalysis within the Macy-sponsored cybernetics conferences, see Heims.

3. In Weaver's and Wiener's writings, and even in Shannon's "The Mathematical Theory of Communication," the terms "communication" and "information" are used interchangeably, though "information" is also used to signify the content of communication. This overlapping of the two terms continues a tendency that was also prevalent before World War II. From a contemporary perspective, it may be objected that these two terms

now signify different events and research fields. Viewed historically, however, they share a common epistemological and social heritage in a "conduit" or transmission model for knowledge and language. Further, one might argue that this common model is still present and easily seen by the ease in which information technologies converge with communications technologies and conversely (for example, in the case of the internet, which is understood as both a communicational and an informational medium). I believe that the issue of defining the differences between "communication" and "information" is less important than that of accounting for their common historical assumptions in practice and theory.

4. For an article examining the extension of the cybernetic communication model to biological entities as a whole, see Haraway.

5. The conduit model is itself a linguistic model for language based on speech. Ferdinand de Saussure, the father of structural linguistics, for example, spoke in his famous "Course in General Linguistics" of the "speaking-circuit" *("le circuit de la parole")* (*Cours de Linguistique Générale* 27), which was formed between two people in the transmission of their ideas through the medium of spoken language. The deconstruction of this "logocentric" model for language and other types of signs, and for philosophy as a whole, is undertaken in Derrida's *Of Grammatology* as well as in other works by Derrida, such as *The Postcard*.

6. Such a view of language as a series of consistent codes also allows for cybernetics' integration of human and technical agents in electronically mediated communication. This view may be seen in some versions of the contemporary discourse on cyborgs, virtuality, and the so-called posthuman. The notion of a "seamless" integration of the technical and the human, though, must be performed at either the biological level or at the social level. If it is performed at the social level, it requires environmental restrictions upon human agency (as in virtual reality environments) or social conditioning (which would aid, for example, ubiquitous computing). Such human conditioning is necessary because electronic "communication" is that of a code, whereas human language is not a code proper. Such a property of human language and being, in general, creates a condition of material resistance that makes "seamless" cyborg integration ontologically problematic (at least where behavioral, rather than biological, action is present). As suggested in this book, Wiener's popular texts might be viewed, at least in part, as political attempts to enact those operational conditions wherein cyborg relationships become more likely, leading to a more "efficient" and "effective" society. Needless to say, such a relationship is not equal: viewed as a whole and according to type (rather than speed), humans are much more adaptable to machine environments than the reverse, because whereas humans can at least mimic machine logic and causality, machines cannot reach the affective range of humans and human language. (Think, for example, how differently silence is understood by a machine [as delay] and by humans [where it can have various affective meanings].) The result is that in a cyborg environment, at least at a level of language and society, humans *must* become operational in the manner of machines in order to create a relatively smooth linkage of codes and procedures between humans and machines. The reverse is conceivable only insomuch as it requires stepped-down translations or countless means of compensating for a loss of human affect (a compensation that artificial intelligence has been, despite fifty years of research, unable to fully account for even in relatively simple cases of language translation or even in the duplication of human physiological movements). Linkage in this direction is anything but smooth or seamless.

7. The following example shows the political anxiety that Wiener held toward problems of language as a whole and his desire to see language regulated by economies of constant exchange value:

> There are vast fields of law where there is no satisfactory semantic agreement between what the law intends to say and the actual situation that it contemplates. Whenever such a theoretical agreement fails to exist, we shall have the same sort of no-man's land that faces us when we have two currency systems without an accepted basis of parity. In the zone of unconformity between one court and another, there is always a refuge for the dishonest middleman, who will accept payment neither financially nor morally except in the system most favorable to him, and will give it only in the system in which he sacrifices least. The greatest opportunity of the criminal in the modern community lies in this position as a dishonest broker in the interstices of the law. (*The **Human** Use of Human Beings* 118)

8. In his 1959 lecture, "The Way to Language" ("Der Weg zur Sprache"), Heidegger makes some very pointed remarks as to the relation of information theory to language. The gist of Heidegger's critique is one that this chapter retraces and that I will investigate in greater detail in the chapter 5. Briefly, Heidegger argues that the metaphysics of modern technology inhabits information theory and the modern concept of information so that language is understood from the beginning as an operationalized event, a conceptualization that then operationalizes human beings through this conception of language. Countering information theory's claim that language (in the form of "the message") begins with the subject's intentions within a rational context of language and communication, Heidegger argues that language is deeply historical and social and that enunciation is a result of listening to what language tells us about the world and then speaking (or writing) out of those possibilities of, and for, language.

9. See chapter 1.2 of Michael Hardt and Antonio Negri's book, *Empire,* for an excellent explication of this point.

10. Agamben discusses the relation of such a concept of community through Marx's notion of "general intellect" (as developed at the end of Marx's *Grundrisse*) in his essay, "Form-of-Life." The notion of "general intellect" plays an important role in recent Italian Autonomous Marxist thought, indicating a form of social production that is, in various degrees, exterior to regulated State economies. In particular, the development of post-Fordist, information-based economies is sometimes pointed to as a possible break from the traditional organization of labor within the capitalist State. The literature on this is large, at least in Italian. One good English language collection, however, is Paolo Virno and Michael Hardt's *Radical Thought in Italy: A Potential Politics.* Since there are various conceptions of the notion of "general intellect" in relation to various notions of production and value, I will not, for fear of losing the critical narrative I have set upon in this chapter, venture further on this important discourse. I will quickly mention, however, that it is possible for a conception of general intellect to be appropriated within terms of a capitalist-dominated information utopianism. It is precisely such a turn, I would suggest, that occurs in Pierre Lévy's discussions of the "virtual." (In examining Otlet's work, an earlier conception of "general intellect" appears in terms of "world mind.") For a reading of general intellect from the aspect of French writers and exiled Italian Autonomists associated with the 1990s journal *Futur Antérieur,* see Dyer-Witheford.

4. Pierre Lévy and the "Virtual"

1. In *Difference and Repetition,* Deleuze seems to posit the idea of virtual unfoldings

or becomings in relation to, but against, a classical understanding of structuralism in the sense of a priori forms or archetypes. For example:

> It is not surprising that, among many of the authors who promote it, *structuralism* is so often accompanied by calls for a new theatre or a new (non-Aristotelian) interpretation of the theatre: a theatre of multiplicities opposed in every respect to the theatre of representation, which leaves intact neither the identity of the thing represented, nor author, nor spectator, nor character, nor representation which, through the vicissitudes of the play, can become the object of a production of knowledge or final recognition. (192)

This model of virtual unfoldings seems to find examples in such events as "linguistic multiplicity" (which Deleuze articulates in terms very similar to that of Chomsky's generative grammar) and genetic expression (193).

2. Daniel Paul Schreber's *Memoirs of My Nervous Disorder* was the basis for Freud's 1911 essay "Psycho-Analytic Notes upon an Autobiographical Account of a Case of Paranoia." The Schreber case is a foundational example in Deleuze and Guattari's *Anti-Oedipus,* and "Schreber" becomes a trope in that text for the oppositional relation of schizoanalysis to classical psychoanalysis and its normative ideals.

3. For example, the psychotic may confuse identification and desire (two concepts that Freud in his writings always struggled to keep distinct from one another in order to preserve the classical Oedipal triangle; see, particularly, Freud's *Group Psychology and the Analysis of the Ego*). See Schreber's schizo-destruction of the Oedipal triangle in his *Memoirs* where the following terms are made conceptually equivalent to one another: sun = father = mother = me = woman that I desire = woman that I am.

4. In philosophy, ethics seems to me to be a nice example of a complex idea that is made present in an actualization that does not solve but, instead, returns again and again to its complex or problematic nature. The discourse of ethics in Western philosophy has been ongoing for at least 2,500 years, but no one would claim that it has solved such issues as that of right and of justice. Looking at philosophical ethics for solutions to ethical problems would be to misunderstand the nature of philosophical ethics. The repetition of problems in philosophical ethics itself constitutes types of answers to ethical problems (e.g., the discussion produces social concern, guilt, shame, awareness, etc.). Of course, such answers *as affects* cannot be characterized in terms of finalization or solution.

5. "Encore une fois, ils ne sont pas totalement indépendants de l'espace-temps de référence, puis-qu'ils doivent toujours se greffer sur des supports physiques et s'actualiser ici ou ailleurs, maintenant ou plus tard" (*Qu'est-ce que le virtuel?* 18).

6. See, for example, Lacan's seminar, *The Ego in Freud's Theory and in the Technique of Psychoanalysis, 1954–1955.*

7. On the temporal construction of *Nachträglichkeit,* see Derrida, "Freud and the Scene of Writing."

8. On the "poetic function" in language, see, for example, Jakobson and also Shklovsky.

9. For an example of this use of the pronominal "I," see the beginning of Barrett Watten's epic poem, "Under Erasure."

10. See Wittgenstein's discussion in *Philosophical Investigations* regarding the grammatical construct "I am in pain" and the like.

11. For critical literature on the encoding of everyday life according to the codes of capitalist production and consumption (particularly through language) and the neces-

sary conditions for this within post-Fordism, see not only Guattari and Alliez but also Marazzi; Marco Revelli's preface to Mario Agostinelli's *Tempo e spazio nell'impresa post-fordista;* and Hardt and Negri. The Italian political condition over the past half-century has left a still-fertile ground for critiques of neo-liberalism's role in fostering a post-Fordist society of control. The Italian literature constitutes an important critical exception to the uncritical verbiage about "virtual" production and organization that dominates Anglo-American and even French writings.

12. For a critique of the liberal tradition's understanding of the concept of money as a transparent medium for exchange, see, for example, Negri's critique (following Marx in the *Grundrisse*) in *Marx Beyond Marx.*

5. Heidegger and Benjamin: The Metaphysics and Fetish of Information

1. For a fuller treatment of some of Heidegger's themes regarding technology in the context of his earlier work, see Fynsk. The issue of technology in Heidegger's later works is treated in Weber. An interesting reading of Heidegger's concerns with technology, especially the communicational aspects of modern technology and its relation to Heidegger's own politics in the 1930s, occurs in Ronell.

2. It is interesting that Heidegger partly marks this transition from scholarship to research work with the advent of public document collections, at least in the form of publishers' series and sets:

> The research man no longer needs a library at home. Moreover, he is constantly on the move. He negotiates at meetings and collects information at congresses. He contracts for commissions with publishers. The latter now determine along with him which books must be written. ("Age of the World Picture" 125)

See also Heidegger's comments in appendix 3 to "The Age of the World Picture" where Heidegger continues this train of thought, accusing the publishing industry of creating a public space of knowledge through selective publishing strategies and the establishment of canons.

3. As will be seen in Benjamin's writings, the construction of experience by industrial modernity remains a central problematic for critics who lean both toward the political right and left during this period in Europe. Benjamin, in his essay on Baudelaire, makes the social construction of "lived experience" (*Erlebnis*) a central issue in his critique of modernity. Needless to say, to speak today of "experience" as a suspect epistemic or social category is as foreign to our sensibilities as it is to do the same with "information." For example, imagine in any way denigrating the value of "experience" or "information" in education in the United States today, especially in light of higher education programs that award academic credit based on "life-experiences." One could perhaps speculate that such a program of knowledge would have been academically inconceivable for Heidegger and deeply politically suspect for Benjamin. For both critics, critical thought must dissolve the representational "aura" of modernity and ideology that frames objects, beings, and events, and this requires a critical relation to phenomena—a critical relation that must pass through historical reassessments and, particularly, through language. Critical thought must rethink the experiences and information that the everyday world seems to freely give in order to become knowledge. (See, for example, Heidegger's comments about the everyday [*Alltäglichkeit*] in *Being and Time,* as well as Benjamin's comments on journalistic information, referred to later in this chapter.) Further, given the difficulty of both

Heidegger's and Benjamin's styles of writing, one may perhaps understand their own writing as both an instance and a performance of this critical struggle against "experience," "information," and "communication." Critical language cannot be "clear and distinct" in the manner connoted by the modern sense of the term "information" if such language has the task of wrestling knowledge *from* information.

4. On the origins of the metaphysical tradition from out of the Latin reinterpretation of Greek philosophy, see, for example, Heidegger's discussion of causation at the beginning of "The Question Concerning Technology."

5. The Paris arcades were iron-and-glass-enclosed shopping "malls" that were built out of boulevards in the mid-nineteenth century and then largely abandoned with the appearance of department stores in the twentieth century. As such, they were among the first specifically designed consumer markets in Paris and, for Benjamin, represented one of the first architecturally designed spaces in Paris for concentrating many of the qualities of modern culture.

6. Benjamin had expressed a similar notion four years earlier in "The Work of Art in the Age of Mechanical Reproduction":

> The film is the art form that is in keeping with the increased threat to his life which modern man has to face. Man's need to expose himself to shock effects is his adjustment to the dangers threatening him. The film corresponds to profound changes in the apperceptive apparatus—changes that are experienced on an individual scale by the man in the street in big-city traffic, on a historical scale by every present-day citizen. (250)

7. A detailed argument on politics as aesthetic spectacle is given in Hewitt. See, particularly, chapter 6 of that book.

8. Evidence of Benjamin's interest in the film, literature, and photography of the Soviet avant-garde dates from his visit to Moscow during the winter of 1926–27 and is present not only in "The Author as Producer" (where Sergei Tretiakov, one of the cofounders of the famous Soviet Left Front of Art and friend of Brecht, is mentioned) but in reviews that Benjamin wrote in the late 1920s through his work in the 1930s and 1940. The importance of the Soviet avant-garde for Benjamin's materialist analysis is, I believe, greater than the number of explicit references in his work would lead one to believe. Without understanding the Soviet avant-garde and its appearance from out of a historical interruption or "caesura" (i.e., the Soviet revolution), one may be led (as I think is the case with many of Benjamin's commentators) to read Benjamin's notions of "interruption" and "montage" in more aesthetically "bourgeois," theoretical, and even mystical manners than I think is warranted by such works as "The Author as Producer."

9. Benjamin's understanding of "montage" as a historical strategy cannot be understood outside of its aesthetic-political foundations. In this regard, it is useful to remember the importance that Benjamin places upon "technique" in montage in his essay "The Author as Producer." There, Benjamin is not advocating montage *itself* as a critical technique but rather montage as a critical technique within the context of "historicism." The history of this engagement between technique and what Benjamin calls historicism can be traced up to the present, for example, in the poetic and critical works of the Language school of poetics in the United States and, in particular, the works of poet and cultural critic Barrett Watten (though Watten's sense of critical engagement goes much beyond the technique of montage proper). I would suggest that the hermeneutic difficulties that occur for many readers in trying to understand the work of the formalist avant-garde,

both historical and contemporary, may be illuminated by a consideration of Benjamin's political project.

10. The relation of aesthetic technique and historical technique for Benjamin is very clear if we examine Benjamin's use of the term *"Abfall."* In Benjamin's *Arcades Project,* section "N," Benjamin notes the need for a materialist historiography to build its critique out of the *"Abfall der Geschichte"* (commonly translated as the "trash of history," but perhaps better translated in the noncolloquial context of Benjamin's texts as "remainder"— hence, the "historical remainder"). Benjamin uses this same term in speaking about the dadaists' critical use of language:

> The Dadaists attached much less importance to the sales value of their work than to its uselessness for contemplative immersion. The studied degradation of their material was not the least of their means to achieve this uselessness. Their poems are "word salad" containing obscenities and every imaginable waste product *[Abfall]* of language. ("Work of Art" 237)

My point is that Benjamin's work, like the dadaists', attempted to construct a social and political critique out of excess to bourgeois taste (here, for history). This example may also illuminate how strongly Benjamin's critique is not *only* "aesthetic" or "historical" or "political" but also, in a very wide sense, "cultural" and how the former categories come together in this last term. Culture, for Benjamin, is political aesthetics, and history is the proliferation of culture in, and over, time.

11. On the concept of historical remainders, see not only section "N" of *The Arcades Project* but also Benjamin's discussion about "outmoded" objects in his essay "Surrealism."

12. Benjamin's work implies not only a critique of progress but of linear historical causality and traditional historiographical narrative as well. Through the aesthetics of interruption, the "now of recognizability" appears, cutting through the continuity of the present and the past by arresting the dialectic whose movement is the means for historical linearity and progress. The "now of recognizability" is, thus, a moment of historical "caesura" (*Arcades Project* [N10a,3] 475)—a caesura that should be understood both historically and historiographically. Benjamin's *"Jetztzeit"* is, thus, not simply a critical presentation of objects of "the past" in relation to "the present" but rather is a critique of modernity and modernist historiography itself, wherein a past-present-future temporal horizon is constructed and is understood in terms of continuity and progress.

6. Conclusion: "Information" and the Role of Critical Theory

1. See the remarks of Theodor Adorno et al. in *The Positivist Dispute in German Sociology* for one reading of critical theory in relation to the quantitative social sciences.

▪ Works Cited

Adorno, Theodor. "Scientific Experiences of a European Scholar in America." *The Intellectual Migration: Europe and America, 1930–1960*. Ed. Donald Fleming and Bernard Bailyn. Cambridge: Harvard UP, 1968. 338–70.

Adorno, Theodor, et al. *The Positivist Dispute in German Sociology*. Trans. Glyn Adey and David Frisby. New York: Harper, 1976.

Agamben, Giorgio. *The Coming Community*. Trans. Michael Hardt. Minneapolis: U of Minnesota P, 1993.

———. "Form-of-Life." *Radical Thought in Italy: A Potential Politics*. Ed. Paolo Virno and Michael Hardt. Trans. Maurizia Boscagli et al. Minneapolis: U of Minnesota P, 1996. 150–56.

Agostinelli, Mario. *Tempo e spazio nell'impresa postfordista*. Preface by Marco Revelli. Rome: Manifestolibri, 1997.

Benjamin, Walter. *The Arcades Project*. Trans. Howard Eiland and Kevin McLaughlin. Cambridge: Harvard UP, 1999.

———. "The Author as Producer." *Reflections: Essays, Aphorisms, Autobiographical Writings*. Ed. Peter Demetz. Trans. Edmund Jephcott. New York: Schocken, 1978. 220–38.

———. "On Some Motifs in Baudelaire." *Illuminations*. Ed. Hannah Arendt. Trans. Harry Zohn. New York: Schocken, 1968. 155–200.

———. "Paris, the Capital of the Nineteenth Century." *The Arcades Project*. Cambridge: Harvard UP, 1999. 3–13.

———. *Das Passagen-Werk*. Ed. Rolf Tiedemann. 2 vols. Frankfurt am Main: Suhrkamp Verlag, 1982.

———. "Surrealism." *Reflections: Essays, Aphorisms, Autobiographical Writings*. Ed. Peter Demetz. Trans. Edmund Jephcott. New York: Schocken, 1978. 177–92.

———. "The Task of the Translator: An Introduction to the Translation of Baudelaire's *Tableaux Parisiens*." *Illuminations*. Ed. Hannah Arendt. Trans. Harry Zohn. New York: Schocken, 1968. 69–82.

———. "Theses on the Philosophy of History." *Illuminations*. Ed. Hannah Arendt. Trans. Harry Zohn. New York: Schocken, 1968. 253–64.

———. "The Work of Art in the Age of Mechanical Reproduction." *Illuminations*. Ed. Hannah Arendt. Trans. Harry Zohn. New York: Schocken, 1968. 217–51.

Borch-Jacobsen, Mikkel. "The Primal Band." *The Emotional Tie: Psychoanalysis, Mimesis, and Affect*. Stanford: Stanford UP, 1993.

Briet, Suzanne. "Bibliothécaires et documentalistes." *Revue de documentation* 21 (1954): 41–45.

———. *Entre Aisne et Meuse . . . et au-delà: souvenirs*. Charleville-Mézières: Société des Écrivains Ardennais, 1976.

———. *Qu'est-ce que la documentation?* Paris: Edit, 1951.

Buckland, Michael K. "The Centenary of 'Madame Documentation': Suzanne Briet, 1894–1989." *Journal of the American Society for Information Science* 46.3 (1995): 235–37.

———. "What Is a 'Document'?" *Journal of the American Society for Information Science* 48.9 (1997): 804–9. Reprinted at: http://www.sims.berkeley.edu/~buckland/whatdoc.html.

Cacaly, Serge, ed. "Otlet, Paul (1868–1944)." *Dictionnaire encyclopédique de l'information et de la documentation.* Paris: Éditions Nathan, 1997. 446–47.

Casey, Marion. "Efficiency, Taylorism, and Libraries in Progressive America." *Journal of Library History* 16 (1981): 265–79.

Deleuze, Gilles. *Difference and Repetition.* Trans. Paul Patton. New York: Columbia UP, 1994.

———. *The Logic of Sense.* Trans. Mark Lester. New York: Columbia UP, 1990.

Deleuze, Gilles, and Félix Guattari. *Anti-Oedipus: Capitalism and Schizophrenia.* Trans. Robert Hurley, Mark Seem, and Helen R. Lane. Minneapolis: U of Minnesota P, 1983.

———. *A Thousand Plateaus: Capitalism and Schizophrenia.* Trans. Brian Massumi. Minneapolis: U of Minnesota P, 1987.

Derrida, Jacques. "Freud and the Scene of Writing." *Writing and Difference.* Chicago: U of Chicago P, 1978. 196–231.

———. *Of Grammatology.* Trans. Gayatri Chakravorty Spivak. Baltimore: John Hopkins UP, 1974.

———. *The Postcard: From Socrates to Freud and Beyond.* Trans. Alan Bass. Chicago: U of Chicago P, 1987.

Dyer-Witheford, Nick. *Cyber-Marx: Cycles and Circuits of Struggle in High-Technology Capitalism.* Urbana: U of Illinois P, 1999.

Edwards, Paul N. *The Closed World: Computers and the Politics of Discourse in Cold War America.* Cambridge: MIT P, 1996.

Foucault, Michel. *The Order of Things: An Archaeology of the Human Sciences.* New York: Random, 1973.

Freud, Sigmund. *Group Psychology and the Analysis of the Ego.* Trans. James Stachey. New York: Norton, 1959.

———. "Psycho-Analytic Notes upon an Autobiographical Account of a Case of Paranoia (Dementia Paranoides)." *Sigmund Freud: Collected Papers, Volume 3.* New York: Basic, 1959. 387–470.

———. *Totem and Taboo: Some Points of Agreement Between the Mental Lives of Savages and Neurotics.* Trans. James Stachey. New York: Norton, 1950.

Fynsk, Christopher. *Heidegger: Thought and Historicity.* Ithaca: Cornell UP, 1986.

Girard, René. *Violence and the Sacred.* Trans. Patrick Gregory. Baltimore: John Hopkins UP, 1977.

Gresleri, Giuliano. "Le Mundaneum: Lecture du Projet." *Le Corbusier à Genève, 1922–1932: projets et réalisations.* Ed. Isabelle Charollais and André Ducret. Lausanne: Payot, 1987. 70–78.

Guattari, Félix. "Desire Is Power, Power Is Desire." *Soft Subversions.* Ed. Sylvère Lotringer. New York: Semiotext(e), 1996. 15–23.

———. "Machinic Heterogenesis." *Chaosmosis: An Ethico-Aesthetic Paradigm.* Trans. Paul Bains and Julian Pefanis. Bloomington: Indiana UP, 1995. 33–57.

———. "On Machines." *Journal of Philosophy and the Visual Arts* 6 (1995): 8–12.

———. "Schizoanalytic Metamodelisation." *Chaosmosis: An Ethico-Aesthetic Paradigm.* Trans. Paul Bains and Julian Pefanis. Bloomington: Indiana UP, 1995. 58–76.

————. "Texts for the Russians." *Poetics Journal* 8 (1989): 3–4.

Guattari, Félix, and Eric Alliez. "Capitalistic Systems, Structures, and Processes." *The Guattari Reader.* Ed. Gary Genosko. Cambridge: Blackwell, 1996. 233–47.

Hahn, Trudi Bellardo, and Michael Buckland, eds. *Historical Studies in Information Science.* Medford, NJ: Information Today, 1998.

Hapke, Thomas. "Wilhelm Ostwald, the 'Brücke' (Bridge), and Connections to Other Bibliographic Activities at the Beginning of the Twentieth Century." *Proceedings of the 1998 Conference on the History and Heritage of Science Information Systems.* Ed. Mary Ellen Bowden, Trudi Bellardo Hahn, and Robert V. Williams. Medford, NJ: Information Today, 1999.

Haraway, Donna J. "The High Cost of Information in Post–World War II Evolutionary Biology: Ergonomics, Semiotics, and the Sociobiology of Communication Systems." *Philosophical Forum* 2.3 (1981–82): 244–78.

Hardt, Michael, and Antonio Negri. *Empire.* Cambridge: Harvard UP, 2000.

Heidegger, Martin. "The Age of the World Picture." *The Question Concerning Technology and Other Essays.* New York: Harper, 1977. 115–54.

————. *Being and Time.* Trans. Joan Stambaugh. Albany: State U of New York P, 1996.

————. "The End of Philosophy and the Task of Thinking." *Basic Writings: From Being and Time (1927) to The Task of Thinking (1964).* Ed. David Farrell Krell. New York: Harper, 1977. 370–92.

————. *Kant and the Problem of Metaphysics.* Trans. Richard Taft. 5th ed. Bloomington: Indiana UP, 1997.

————. "Kant's Thesis about Being." *Pathmarks.* Ed. William McNeill. New York: Cambridge UP, 1998. 337–63.

————. "The Question Concerning Technology." *The Question Concerning Technology and Other Essays.* New York: Harper, 1977. 3–35.

————. "The Way to Language." *On the Way to Language.* Trans. Peter D. Hertz. New York: Harper, 1971. 111–36.

Heims, Steve Joshua. *Constructing a Social Science for Postwar America: The Cybernetics Group, 1946–1953.* Cambridge: MIT P, 1993.

Hewitt, Andrew. *Fascist Modernism: Aesthetics, Politics, and the Avant-Garde.* Stanford: Stanford UP, 1993.

Jakobson, Roman. "The Dominant." *Readings in Russian Poetics: Formalist and Structuralist Views.* Ed. Ladislav Matejka and Krystyna Pomorska. Cambridge: MIT P, 1971. 81–87.

Lacan, Jacques. *The Ego in Freud's Theory and in the Technique of Psychoanalysis, 1954–1955.* Trans. Sylvana Tomaselli. New York: Norton, 1988.

Latour, Bruno. "Ces réseaux que la raison ignore: laboratoires, bibliothèques, collections." *Le pouvoir des bibliothèques: la mémoire des livres en Occident.* Ed. Marc Baratin and Christian Jacob. Paris: Albin Michel, 1996. 23–46.

————. *We Have Never Been Modern.* Trans. Catherine Porter. Cambridge: Harvard UP, 1993.

Lévy, Pierre. *Becoming Virtual: Reality in the Digital Age.* Trans. Robert Bononno. New York: Plenum, 1998.

————. *Collective Intelligence: Mankind's Emerging World in Cyberspace.* Trans. Robert Bononno. New York: Plenum, 1997.

————. *L'Intelligence Collective: Pour une anthropologie du cyberspace.* Paris: Éditions La Découverte, 1995.

————. *Qu'est-ce que le virtuel?* Paris: Éditions La Découverte, 1995.

Marazzi, Christian. "Produzione di merci a mezzo di linguaggio." *Stato e diritti nel postfordismo.* Rome: Manifestolibri, 1997. 9–30.

Massumi, Brian. *A User's Guide to Capitalism and Schizophrenia: Deviations from Deleuze and Guattari.* Cambridge: MIT P, 1992.

Nancy, Jean-Luc. "The Inoperative Community." *The Inoperative Community.* Ed. Peter Connor. Trans. Peter Connor, Lisa Garbus, Michael Holland, and Simona Sawhney. Minneapolis: U of Minnesota P, 1991. 1–42.

Negri, Antonio. *Marx Beyond Marx: Lessons on the Grundrisse.* Trans. Harry Cleaver, Michael Ryan, and Maurizio Viano. South Hadley, MA: Bergin, 1984.

Otlet, Paul. *Monde: Essai d'universalisme: Connaissance du monde, sentiment du monde, action organisée et plan du monde.* Brussels: Éditiones Mundaneum, 1935.

————. *Traité de documentation: le livre sur le livre: théorie et pratique.* Brussels: Éditiones Mundaneum, 1934.

Pagès, Robert. "Transformations documentaires et milieu culturel (Essai de documentologie)." *Revue de Documentation* 15 (1948): 53–64.

Rayward, W. Boyd. "H. G. Wells's Idea of a World Brain: A Critical Reassessment." *Journal of the American Society for Information Science* 50.7 (1999): 557–73.

————. "The International Exposition and the World Documentation Congress, Paris, 1937." *Library Quarterly* 53 (1983): 254–68.

————. "The Origins of Information Science and the International Institute of Bibliography/International Federation for Information and Documentation (FID)." *Journal of the American Society for Information Science* 48.4 (1997): 289–300.

————. *The Universe of Information: The Work of Paul Otlet for Documentation and International Organisation.* Moscow: VINITI, 1975.

Reddy, Michael J. "The Conduit Metaphor—A Case of Frame Conflict in Our Language about Language." *Metaphor and Thought.* Ed. Andrew Ortony. 2d ed. New York: Cambridge UP, 1993. 164–201.

Ronell, Avital. *The Telephone Book: Technology, Schizophrenia, Electric Speech.* Lincoln: U of Nebraska P, 1989.

Saussure, Ferdinand de. *Cours de Linguistique Générale.* Paris: Payot, 1949.

Serres, Michel. *The Parasite.* Trans. Lawrence R. Schehr. Baltimore: Johns Hopkins UP, 1982.

Shannon, Claude E., and Warren Weaver. *The Mathematical Theory of Communication.* Illini Books edition. Urbana: U of Illinois P, 1949; 1963.

Shklovsky, Victor. "Art as Technique." *Russian Formalist Criticism: Four Essays.* Lincoln: U of Nebraska P, 1965. 3–57.

Virno, Paolo, and Michael Hardt, eds. *Radical Thought in Italy: A Potential Politics.* Trans. Maurizia Boscagli et al. Minneapolis: U of Minnesota P, 1996.

Watten, Barrett. *Under Erasure.* La Laguna, Canary Islands: Zasterle, 1991.

Weber, Samuel. *Mass Mediauras: Form Technics Media.* Stanford: Stanford UP, 1996.

Wiener, Norbert. *Cybernetics: Or Control and Communication in the Animal and the Machine.* 2d ed. Cambridge: MIT P, 1961.

————. *The **Human** Use of Human Beings: Cybernetics and Society.* Cambridge: Riverside, 1950.

————. *The Human Use of Human Beings: Cybernetics and Society.* New York: Houghton, 1954. New York: Da Capo, 1988.

Wittgenstein, Ludwig. *Philosophical Investigations.* Trans. G. E. M. Anscombe. Oxford: Blackwell, 1967.

▪ Index

Compiled by Nancy Chapo and Robert M. Bristow

Ronald E. Day is an assistant professor in the Library and Information Science Program at Wayne State University. He has published articles on the history, philosophy, and political economy of information.